Contents

Printing

Grammar and Reading

Social Studies

Science

Art

About WE

WE is a movement that brings people together, and gives them the tools to change the world. Our unique family of organizations empowers people at home, around the world, and with our social enterprise. With **WE Charity**, we empower domestic and international change; with **ME to WE**, we create socially conscious products and experiences.

Get involved as a family

You can join the WE Movement as a family—bonding together and building lasting memories as you rally around causes that matter to you. WE provides the inspiration, resources, and support you need to take action as a family, helping you raise caring and compassionate children. There are many ways you can participate in the WE movement, and make giving back a part of your family life. Your family can learn more about the lives of youth in developing communities, raise awareness or funds for social issues, volunteer in your community or on a life-changing trip overseas—and so much more!

Get involved at school

Live WE at school by getting involved as a class volunteering, fundraising, or raising awareness around causes that matter. We can all make a positive impact! The WE Schools program provides education resources and service campaigns, helping students further their curricular learning and develop the life skills for success. WE Schools resources are free to schools and are always evolving to keep the learning materials fresh and relevant. For teachers, it revitalizes their class, the curriculum, and everyone's passion.

Join the Movement

Being empowered to change the world is what the WE Movement is all about. Taking the pledge on WE.org is where it all begins. Join us. We can't change the world without you.

The WE Pledge

I pledge to live WE by making a difference every day. We know that change starts with each of us and that together, we will change the world.

Craig and Marc Kielburger

Humanitarians, activists and social entrepreneurs, brothers Craig and Marc Kielburger believe that together, WE can change the world. Over 20 years ago, they set out on a bold mission: to work with developing communities to free children and their families from poverty and exploitation. Their vision expanded to include empowering youth at home, connecting them with global issues and social causes, and partnering with schools to inspire young change-makers from within the classroom. And with the launch of ME to WE, they created an innovative social enterprise that provides products that make an impact, empowering people to change the world with their everyday consumer choices.

Number Words

1. Trace the numbers and the number words.
   Draw a line to match the numbers to the counters.

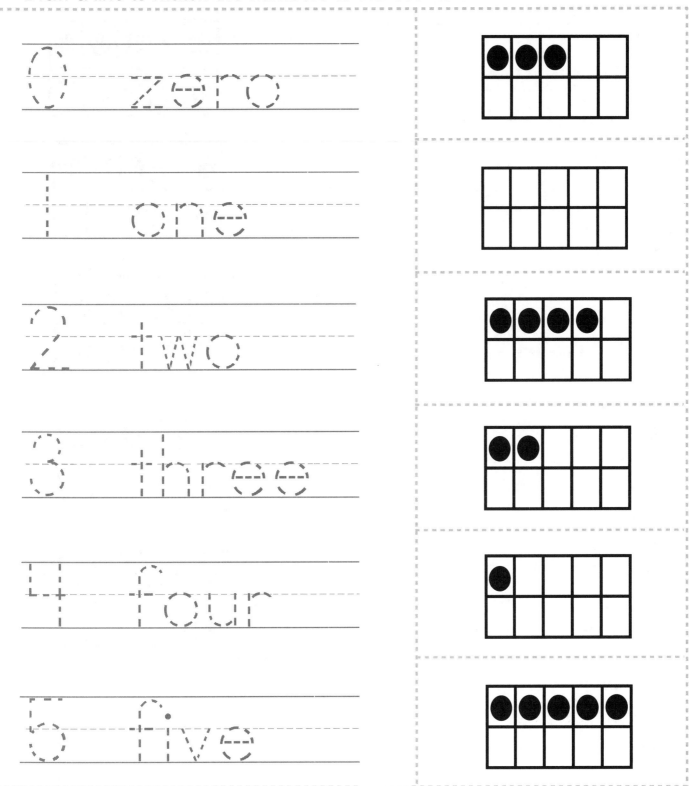

2. Trace the numbers and the number words.
   Draw a line to match the numbers to the counters.

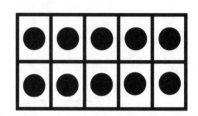

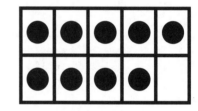

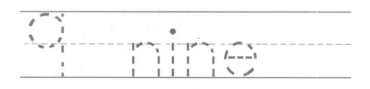

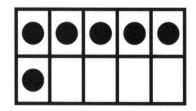

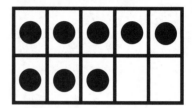

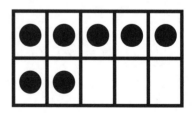

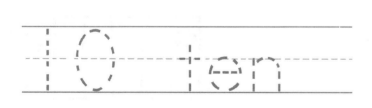

3. How old are you?

_____

- -

_____

Numbers

1. Trace the numbers. Draw ●s to show each number.

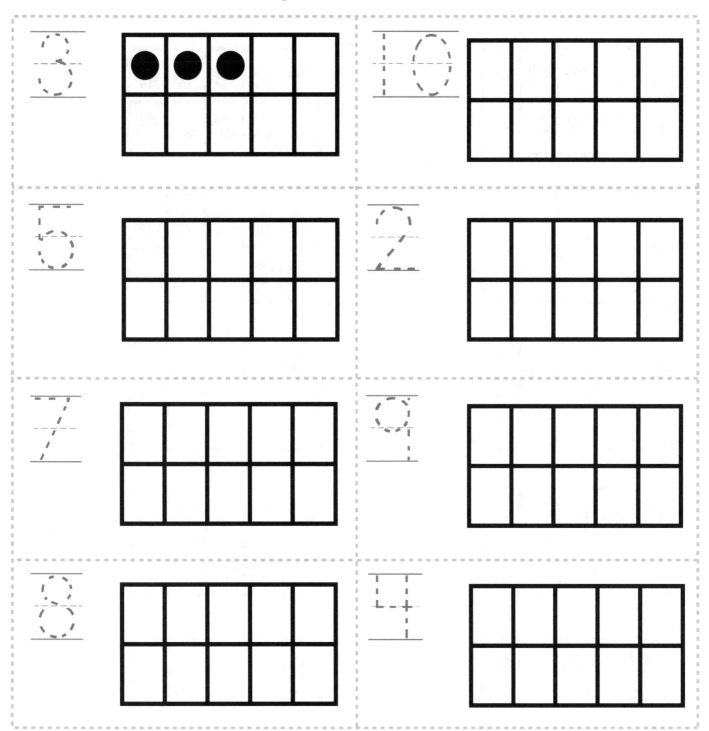

Using Ten-Frames to Count to 10

1. How many counters are there?

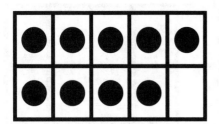 _____

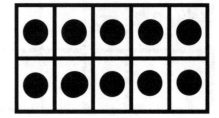 _____

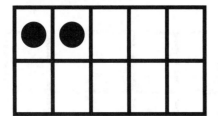 _____

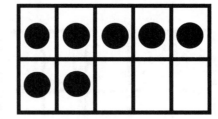 _____

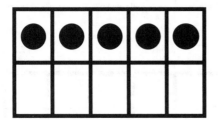 _____

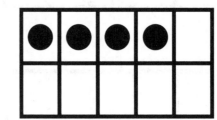 _____

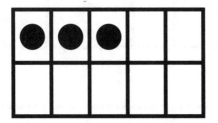 _____

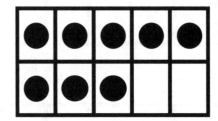 _____

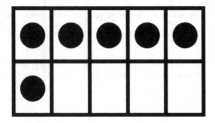 _____

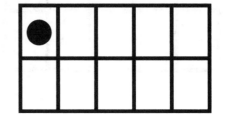 _____

Comparing Numbers from 1 to 10

Compare numbers by counting.

3 is **less than** 5

4 is **greater than** 2

9 is **equal to** 9

1. Compare the numbers. Write the words **greater than, less than,** or **equal to**.

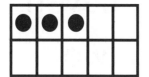 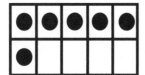

3 is _____ 6

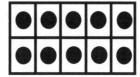 

10 is _____ 8

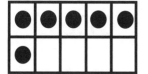 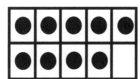

6 is _____ 9

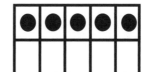 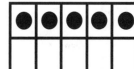

5 is _____ 5

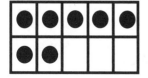 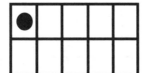

7 is _____ 1

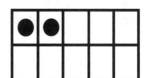

4 is _____ 2

Numbers and Number Words

1. Draw a line from the number to the number word.

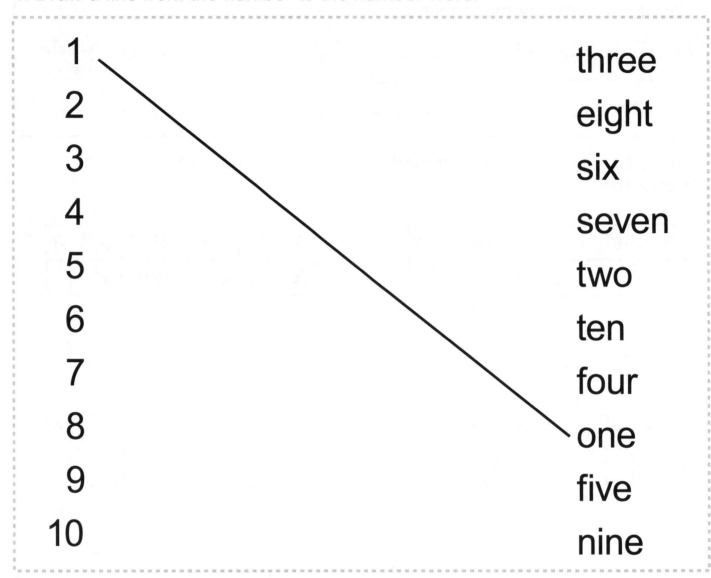

1	three
2	eight
3	six
4	seven
5	two
6	ten
7	four
8	one
9	five
10	nine

BRAIN STRETCH

1. What is the number word for 3? Circle the correct answer.

three   four   two

2. What is the number word for 7? Circle the correct answer.

six   five   seven

Number Words Word Search

1. Circle the correct words in the word search. Cross words off the list when you find them.

z	a	e	i	g	h	t	e
e	w	o	n	e	a	c	h
r	t	s	n	i	n	e	s
o	m	e	u	q	t	w	o
n	f	v	t	h	r	e	e
a	o	e	c	g	o	t	s
s	u	n	f	i	v	e	i
t	r	w	a	t	e	n	x

one   four   seven   ten

two   five   eight   zero

three   six   nine

Counting, Then Writing the Number

1. Look at the picture. How many of each creature? Write the number in the box below the creature.

More, Fewer, and Less

1. Circle the correct set. Write **more** or **fewer**.

a) Circle the set that has **fewer**.

1 is **fewer** than 2.

b) Circle the set that has **more** creatures.

 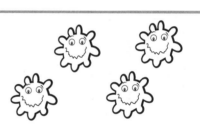

_____ is _____ than _____.

c) Circle the set that has **fewer** creatures.

_____ is _____ than _____.

d) Circle the set that has **more** creatures.

_____ is _____ than _____.

More, Fewer, and Less (continued)

2. Draw to show more or fewer shapes.

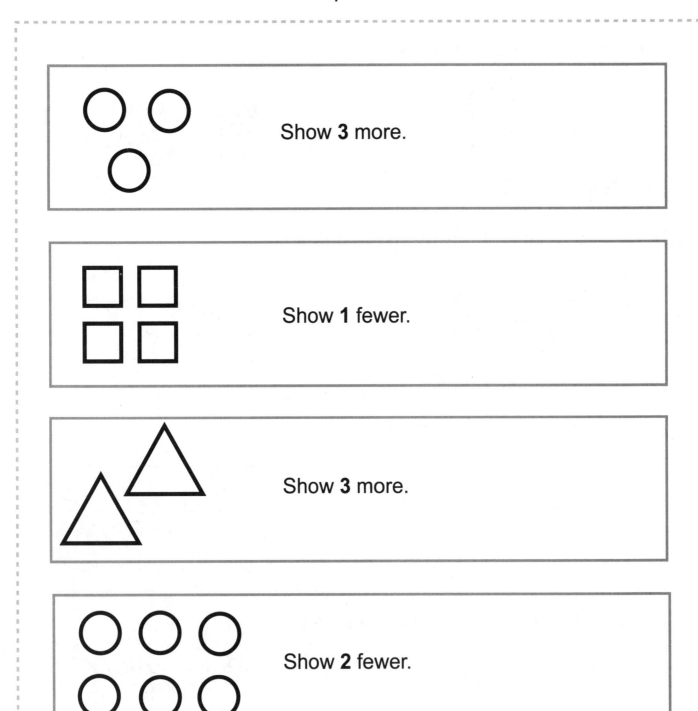

Using Ten-Frames to Count to 20

1. How many counters are there?

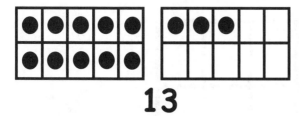

13
_____

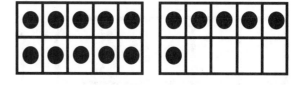
_____

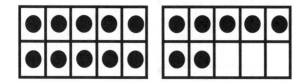
_____

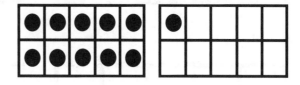
_____

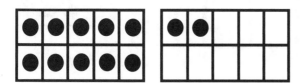
_____

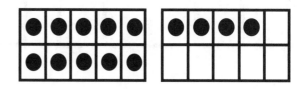
_____

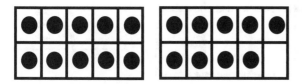
_____

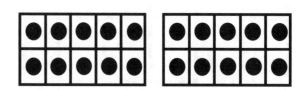
_____

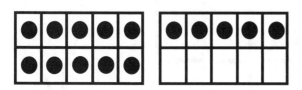
_____

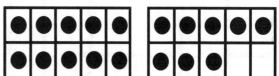
_____

2. Draw ●s in the ten-frames to equal the number.

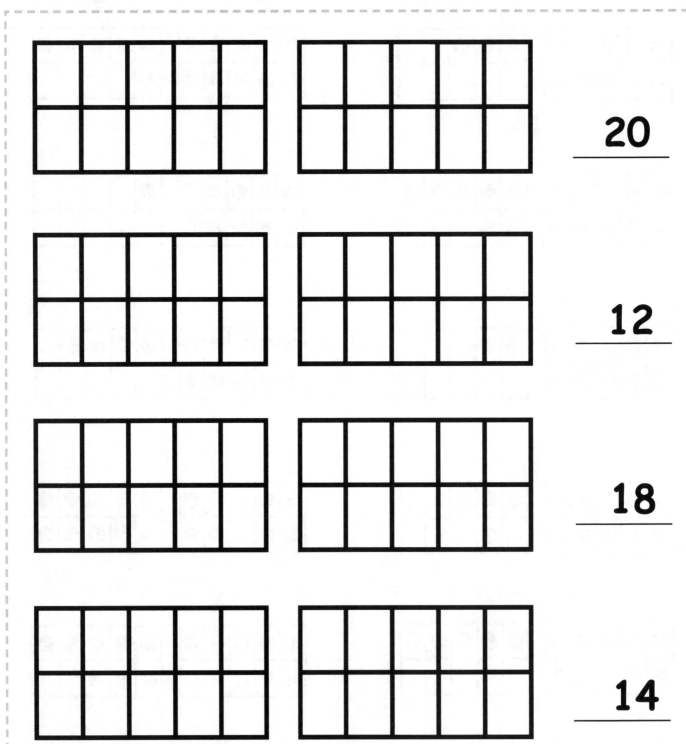

Using Ten-Frames to Count to 20 (continued)

3. Draw 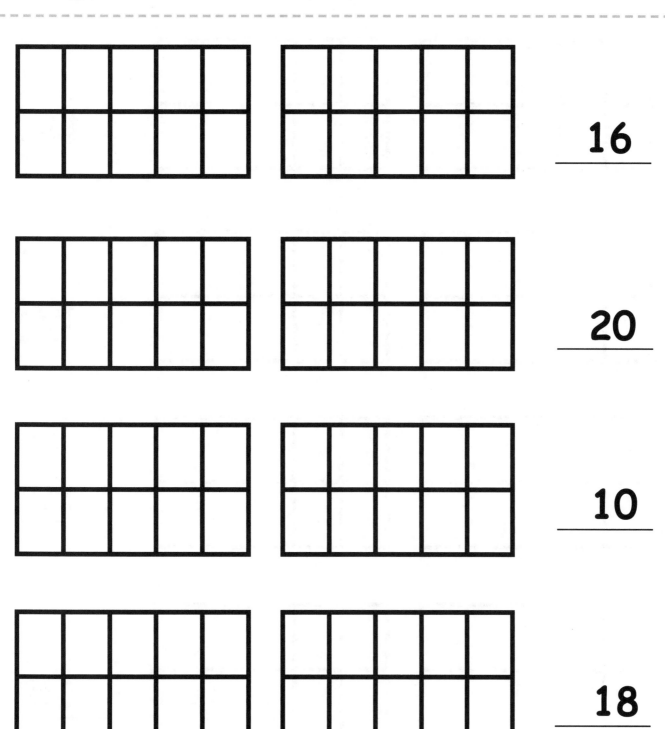●s in the ten-frames to equal the number.

16

20

10

18

4. Draw ●s in the ten-frames to equal the number.

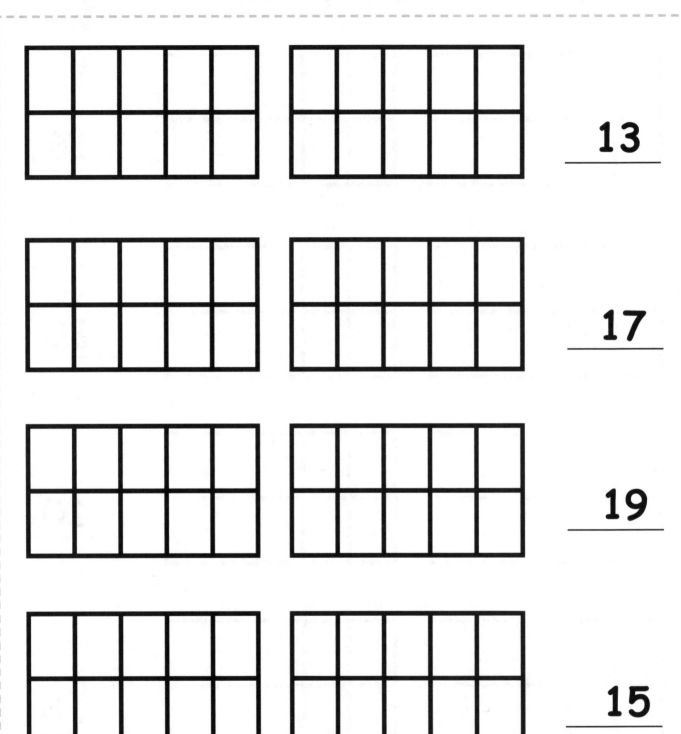

13

17

19

15

Skip Counting by 2s to 30

Connect the dots by skip counting by 2s from 0 to 30. Count out loud.

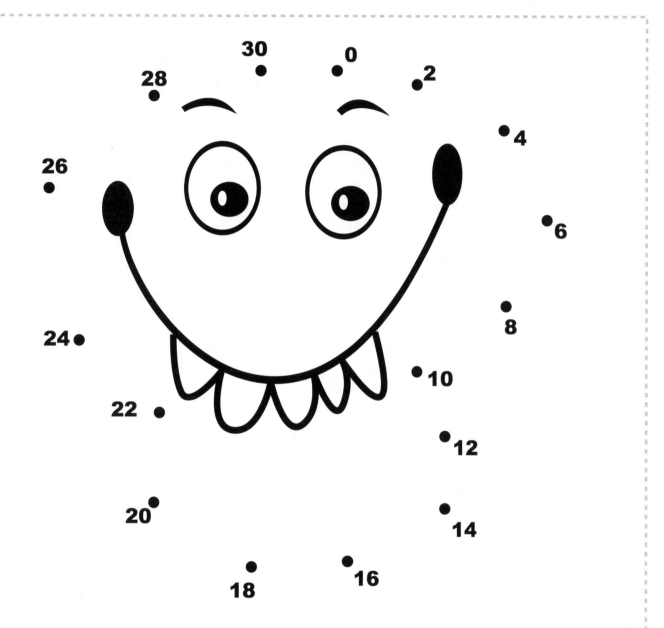

1. Give the creature a name. _____

2. What makes the creature special? _____

Ordering Numbers

1. Fill in the missing numbers. Use the number line to help you.

0 1 2 3 4 5 6 7 8 9 10 11 12 13 14 15 16 17 18 19 20

Just before: _____ , 11, 12

Just before: _____ , 7, 8

Just after: 16, 17, _____

Just before and after: _____ , 13, _____

Between: 9, _____ , 11

Just after: 10, 11, _____

Just before and after: _____ , 17, _____

Between: 18, _____ , 20

Just after: 4, 5, _____

Just before: _____ , 9, 10

BRAIN STRETCH

Name the number just after 11, 12, and 13. Circle your answer.

19   14   10

Skip Counting by 5s to 100

Connect the dots by skip counting by 5s to 100. Count out loud.

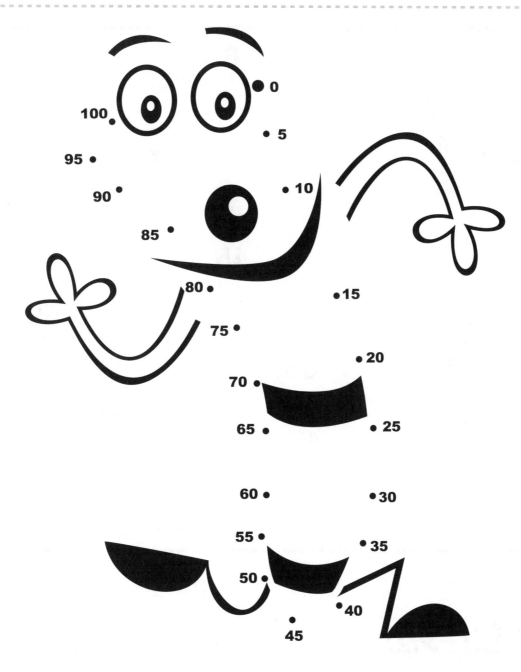

1. Give the creature a name. _____

2. What makes the creature special? _____

Counting to 100

1. Fill in the missing numbers on the chart.

1					6				10
		13							
	22					27			
									40
			44		46				
51								59	
		63		65					
	72						78		80
81						86			
	93						97		100

BRAIN STRETCH

How many legs do one chicken and one horse have in all? Show your thinking.

_____ + _____ = _____

Skip Counting by 10s to 100

Connect the dots by skip counting by 10s to 100. Count out loud.

1. Give the creature a name. _____

2. What makes the creature special? _____

BRAIN STRETCH

How many days are there in a year? _____

How many years are there in a decade? _____

How many years are there in a century? _____

Ordinal Numbers to 10

An ordinal number tells the position of something in a list.

1. Read the ordinal numbers. Underline the part that is the same.

first	second	third	fourth	fifth	sixth	seventh	eighth	ninth	tenth
1st	2nd	3rd	4th	5th	6th	7th	8th	9th	10th

a) The is _____ in line.

b) The is _____ in line.

c) The is _____ in line.

d) The is _____ in line.

e) The is _____ in line.

f) The is _____ in line.

g) The is _____ in line.

2. Circle the correct answer.

a) Who is last?

b) Who is third?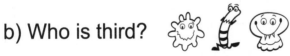

c) Who is between the 2nd and 4th creatures?

Groups of Ten

Circle the groups of ten. Count the ones left over. How many in all?

1.

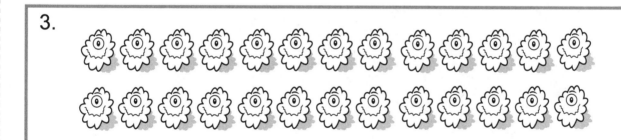

How many groups of 10? _____   How many left over? _____   How many in all? _____

2.

How many groups of 10? _____   How many left over? _____   How many in all? _____

3.

How many groups of 10? _____   How many left over? _____   How many in all? _____

Groups of Ten (continued)

Circle the groups of ten. Count the ones left over. How many in all?

4.

How many groups of 10? _____   How many left over? _____   How many in all? _____

5.

How many groups of 10? _____   How many left over? _____   How many in all? _____

6.

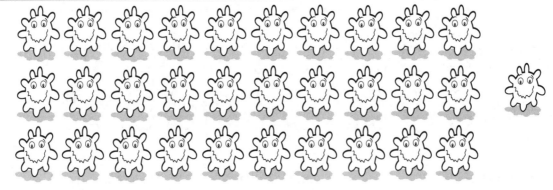

How many groups of 10? _____   How many left over? _____   How many in all? _____

Tens and Ones

Count the tens and ones. Write how many blocks in all.

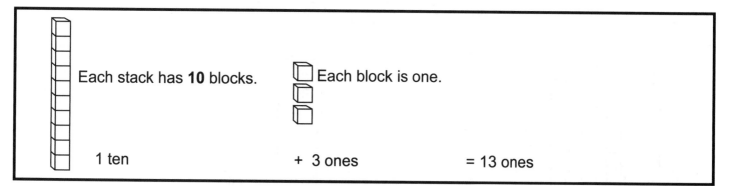

Each stack has **10** blocks.   Each block is one.

1 ten   + 3 ones   = 13 ones

1.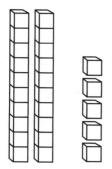

_____ tens + _____ ones = _____ ones

2.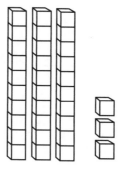

_____ tens + _____ ones = _____ ones

3.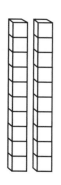

_____ tens + _____ ones = _____ ones

4.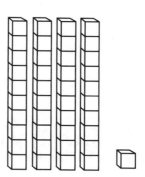

_____ tens + _____ one = _____ ones

Count the tens and ones. Write how many blocks in all.

5.

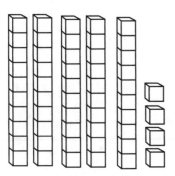

_____ tens + _____ ones = _____ ones

6.

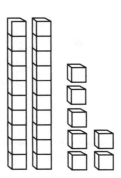

_____ tens + _____ ones = _____ ones

7.

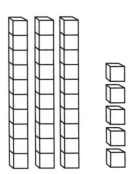

_____ tens + _____ ones = _____ ones

8.

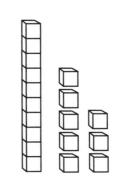

_____ ten + _____ ones = _____ ones

BRAIN STRETCH

Draw the blocks for 2 tens and 3 ones.
What is the number?

Sums to 5

1. Use the blocks to complete the addition sentences.

1 + 3 = **4**

↑ plus   ↑ equals   ↑ sum

4 + 1 = _____

1 + 2 = _____

3 + 1 = _____

2 + 1 = _____

1 + 4 = _____

3 + 2 = _____

1 + 1 = _____

2 + 2 = _____

2 + 3 = _____

2. Draw s to help you add.

● ● ● ● ●

3 + 2 = __5__

1 + 2 = ____

4 + 1 = ____

2 + 2 = ____

1 + 1 = ____

1 + 3 = ____

2 + 3 = ____

3 + 1 = ____

1 + 4 = ____

2 + 1 = ____

Sums to 5 (continued)

3. Use the key to colour the picture.

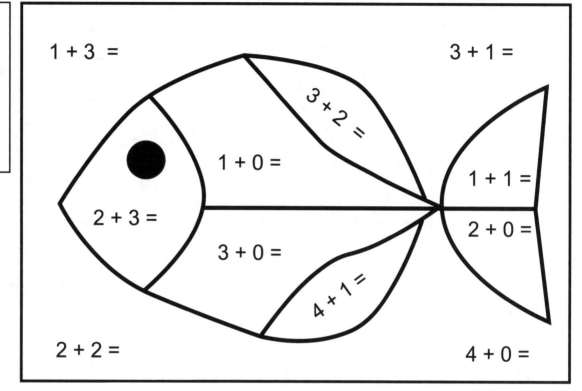

Colour Key
1 – yellow
2 – orange
3 – green
4 – blue
5 – red

1 + 3 =

3 + 1 =

3 + 2 =

1 + 0 =

1 + 1 =

2 + 3 =

3 + 0 =

2 + 0 =

4 + 1 =

2 + 2 =

4 + 0 =

4. Complete the sums.

4 + 1 = ____   3 + 1 = ____   1 + 1 = ____

2 + 0 = ____   5 + 0 = ____   2 + 3 = ____

1 + 3 = ____   0 + 1 = ____   0 + 5 = ____

2 + 2 = ____   1 + 4 = ____   2 + 1 = ____

1 + 0 = ____   3 + 2 = ____   4 + 0 = ____

0 + 4 = ____   1 + 2 = ____   0 + 2 = ____

Addition Facts for 2, 3, 4, and 5

1. Use the key to colour the picture.

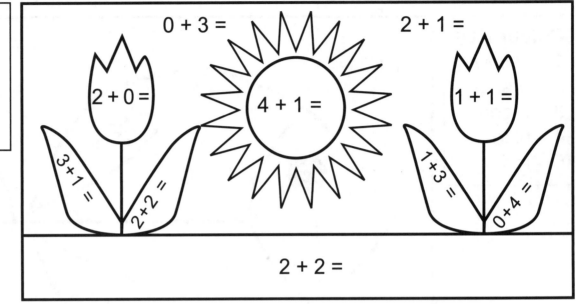

Colour Key
2 – red
3 – blue
4 – green
5 – yellow

0 + 3 =
2 + 1 =
2 + 0 =
4 + 1 =
1 + 1 =
3 + 1 =
2 + 2 =
1 + 3 =
0 + 4 =
2 + 2 =

2. Complete the facts.

0 + 5 = ___   1 + 1 = ___   4 + 0 = ___

1 + 2 = ___   4 + 1 = ___   2 + 0 = ___

1 + 4 = ___   0 + 4 = ___   2 + 3 = ___

0 + 3 = ___   2 + 2 = ___   0 + 2 = ___

3 + 2 = ___   3 + 1 = ___   5 + 0 = ___

2 + 1 = ___   1 + 3 = ___   3 + 0 = ___

Addition Facts for 6, 7, 8, and 9

1. Use the key to colour the picture.

Colour Key
6 – red
7 – blue
8 – green
9 – yellow

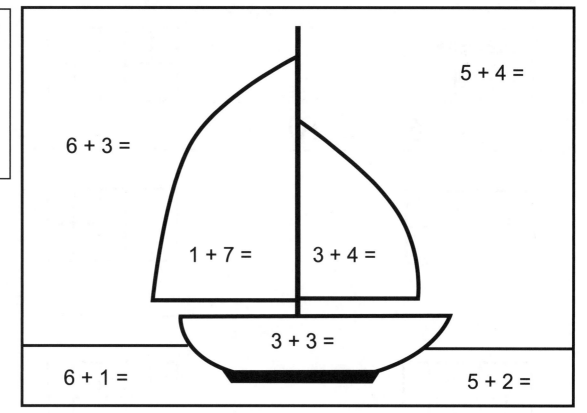

5 + 4 =

6 + 3 =

1 + 7 =   3 + 4 =

3 + 3 =

6 + 1 =   5 + 2 =

2. Complete the facts.

1 + 5 = ___   2 + 6 = ___   3 + 4 = ___

0 + 9 = ___   2 + 5 = ___   0 + 8 = ___

1 + 7 = ___   4 + 5 = ___   2 + 7 = ___

0 + 6 = ___   3 + 5 = ___   0 + 7 = ___

1 + 6 = ___   3 + 3 = ___   4 + 4 = ___

4 + 2 = ___   1 + 8 = ___   2 + 4 = ___

How Many Ways Can You Make 10?

Use the ten-frames to make 10. Use two different colours. Then, write the answers.

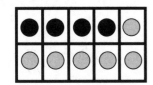

$$\underline{}4 + \underline{}6 = \underline{}10$$

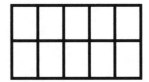

$$\underline{} + \underline{} = \underline{}$$

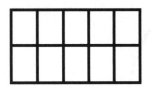

$$\underline{} + \underline{} = \underline{}$$

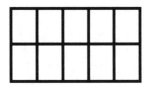

$$\underline{} + \underline{} = \underline{}$$

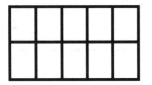

$$\underline{} + \underline{} = \underline{}$$

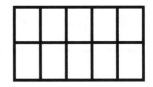

$$\underline{} + \underline{} = \underline{}$$

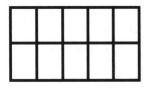

$$\underline{} + \underline{} = \underline{}$$

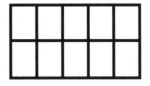

$$\underline{} + \underline{} = \underline{}$$

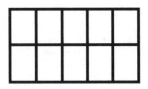

$$\underline{} + \underline{} = \underline{}$$

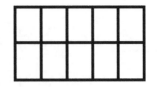

$$\underline{} + \underline{} = \underline{}$$

Addition Practice—Sums Up to 10

1. Write the number sentence.

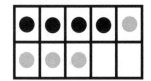

__4__ + __4__ = __8__

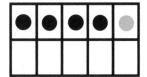

_____ + _____ = _____

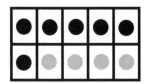

_____ + _____ = _____

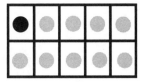

_____ + _____ = _____

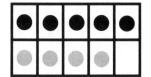

_____ + _____ = _____

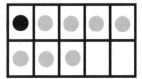

_____ + _____ = _____

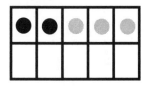

_____ + _____ = _____

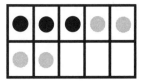

_____ + _____ = _____

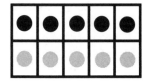

_____ + _____ = _____

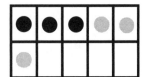

_____ + _____ = _____

2. Write the number sentence.

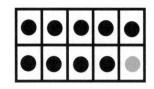

_____ + _____ = _____

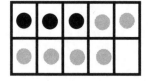

_____ + _____ = _____

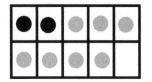

_____ + _____ = _____

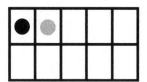

_____ + _____ = _____

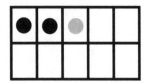

_____ + _____ = _____

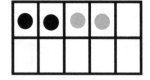

_____ + _____ = _____

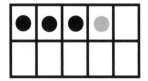

_____ + _____ = _____

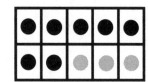

_____ + _____ = _____

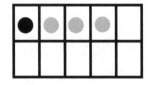

_____ + _____ = _____

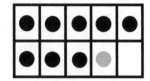

_____ + _____ = _____

Adding 1 or 2 by Counting On

Add 1 by counting on.	**Add 2 by counting on.**
4 + 1 = _____	4 + 2 = _____
Start with the greater number.	Start with the greater number.
Count on by 1.	Count on by 2.
4　　　　5	4　　　　5　　　　6
Stop when 1 finger is up.	Stop when 2 fingers are up.
4 + 1 = **5**	4 + 2 = **6**

1. Count on to add.

7 + 1 = _____ 7, _____	3 + 2 = _____ 3, _____, _____
1 + 1 = _____ 1, _____	8 + 2 = _____ 8, _____, _____
6 + 1 = _____ 6, _____	2 + 2 = _____ 2, _____, _____
5 + 1 = _____ 5, _____	5 + 2 = _____ 5, _____, _____

Adding 1 or 2 by Counting On (continued)

2. Count on to add.

9 + 1 = _____

9, _____

0 + 2 = _____

0, _____, _____

8 + 1 = _____

8, _____

7 + 2 = _____

7, _____, _____

4 + 1 = _____

4, _____

9 + 2 = _____

9, _____, _____

0 + 1 = _____

0, _____

5 + 2 = _____

5, _____, _____

6 + 1 = _____

6, _____

1 + 2 = _____

1, _____, _____

2 + 1 = _____

2, _____

4 + 2 = _____

4, _____, _____

Using a Number Line to Add

Use a number line to add.

6 + 3 = **9**

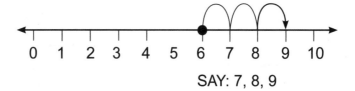

SAY: 7, 8, 9

Mark a dot at 6.
Draw 3 jumps to count on.
Stop at 9.

1. Use the number line to add. Mark a dot to show where to start.
   Next, count on by drawing the jumps. Write the answer.

4 + 3 = ____

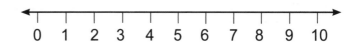

1 + 8 = ____

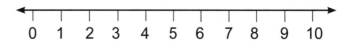

3 + 3 = ____

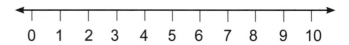

2 + 4 = ____

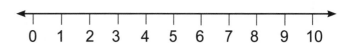

8 + 2 = ____

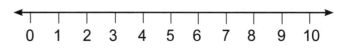

2. Use the number line to add by counting on. Mark a dot to show where to start. Next, draw the jumps. Write the answer.

5 + 4 = _____

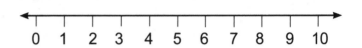

9 + 1 = _____

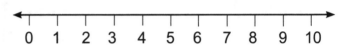

2 + 6 = _____

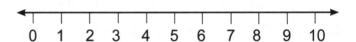

3 + 6 = _____

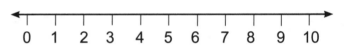

4 + 4 = _____

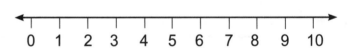

0 + 8 = _____

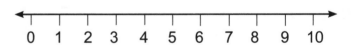

1 + 7 = _____

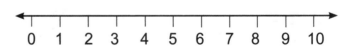

0 + 7 = _____

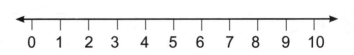

Making Addition Sentences

1. Show three ways to make each number. Use two colours to colour the blocks.

___ + ___ = 9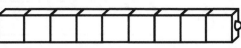

___ + ___ = 9

___ + ___ = 9

___ + ___ = 3

___ + ___ = 3

___ + ___ = 3

___ + ___ = 7

___ + ___ = 7

___ + ___ = 7

___ + ___ = 5

___ + ___ = 5

___ + ___ = 5

Making Addition Sentences (continued)

2. Show three ways to make each number. Use two colours to colour the blocks

___ + ___ = 10

___ + ___ = 10

___ + ___ = 10

___ + ___ = 8

___ + ___ = 8

___ + ___ = 8

___ + ___ = 6

___ + ___ = 6

___ + ___ = 6

___ + ___ = 4

___ + ___ = 4

___ + ___ = 4

Addition Facts to 10

1. Draw a line from the number sentence to the correct answer.

5 + 3 =	3	1 + 2 =
2 + 3 =	**8**	8 + 1 =
6 + 3 =	1	2 + 5 =
1 + 1 =	10	0 + 2 =
3 + 0 =	2	1 + 4 =
5 + 5 =	9	0 + 1 =
1 + 0 =	5	1 + 3 =
4 + 3 =	4	2 + 4 =
3 + 3 =	6	3 + 7 =
2 + 2 =	7	4 + 4 =

BRAIN STRETCH

4 + 1 + 5 =   7 + 2 + 1 =

Differences to 5

1. Count the blocks, then cross them out to finish the subtraction number sentences.

3 − 1 = __2__

  ↑   ↑   ↑
minus   equals difference

5 − 4 = _____

4 − 1 = _____

2 − 1 = _____

4 − 2 = _____

5 − 2 = _____

5 − 3 = _____

5 − 1 = _____

4 − 3 = _____

3 − 2 = _____

2. Draw s, then cross them out to help you subtract.

$5 - 2 = \underline{\textbf{3}}$

$1 - 1 = \underline{\qquad}$

$3 - 2 = \underline{\qquad}$

$5 - 1 = \underline{\qquad}$

$4 - 3 = \underline{\qquad}$

$3 - 1 = \underline{\qquad}$

$5 - 4 = \underline{\qquad}$

$4 - 2 = \underline{\qquad}$

$5 - 3 = \underline{\qquad}$

$4 - 1 = \underline{\qquad}$

Differences to 5 (continued)

3. Subtract. Use the key to colour the picture.

Colour Key
0 – red
1 – blue
2 – green
3 – orange
4 – purple
5 – yellow

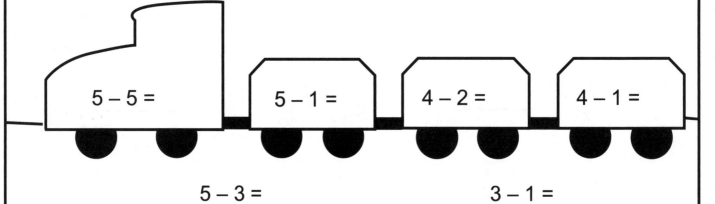

5 – 0 =

5 – 4 =

5 – 5 =

5 – 1 =

4 – 2 =

4 – 1 =

5 – 3 =

3 – 1 =

4. Subtract.

3 – 3 = _____   2 – 1 = _____   5 – 4 = _____

2 – 0 = _____   2 – 2 = _____   4 – 3 = _____

3 – 2 = _____   1 – 1 = _____   4 – 2 = _____

5 – 2 = _____   1 – 0 = _____   4 – 4 = _____

4 – 0 = _____   3 – 0 = _____   5 – 1 = _____

Subtraction Practice

1. Write the number sentence.

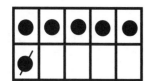

___6___ – ___1___ = ___5___

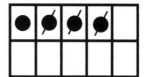

_____ – _____ = _____

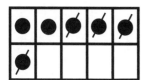

_____ – _____ = _____

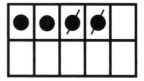

_____ – _____ = _____

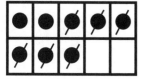

_____ – _____ = _____

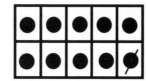

_____ – _____ = _____

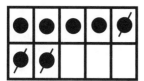

_____ – _____ = _____

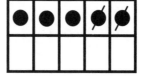

_____ – _____ = _____

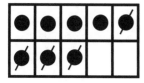

_____ – _____ = _____

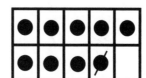

_____ – _____ = _____

Subtraction Practice (continued)

2. Write the number sentence.

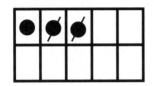

_____ – _____ = _____

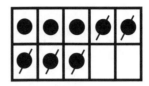

_____ – _____ = _____

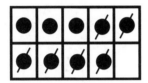

_____ – _____ = _____

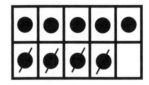

_____ – _____ = _____

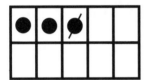

_____ – _____ = _____

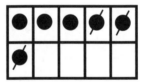

_____ – _____ = _____

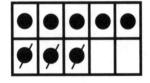

_____ – _____ = _____

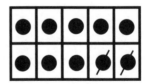

_____ – _____ = _____

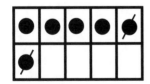

_____ – _____ = _____

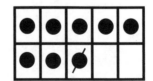

_____ – _____ = _____

How Many Ways Can You Subtract from 10?

1. Use the ten frames to show different ways to subtract from 10.

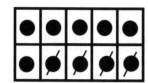

<u>**10**</u> – <u>**4**</u> = <u>**6**</u>

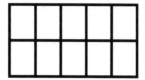

<u>10</u> – <u>　</u> = <u>　</u>

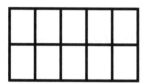

<u>10</u> – <u>　</u> = <u>　</u>

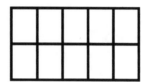

<u>10</u> – <u>　</u> = <u>　</u>

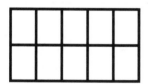

<u>10</u> – <u>　</u> = <u>　</u>

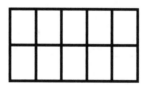

<u>10</u> – <u>　</u> = <u>　</u>

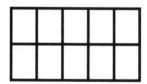

<u>10</u> – <u>　</u> = <u>　</u>

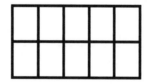

<u>10</u> – <u>　</u> = <u>　</u>

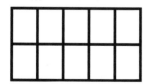

<u>10</u> – <u>　</u> = <u>　</u>

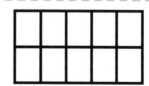

<u>10</u> – <u>　</u> = <u>　</u>

Subtracting 1 or 2 by Counting Back

Subtract 1 by counting back.

3 – 1 = _____

Count back from the first number.

Count out loud.

3   2

Stop when 1 finger is up.

3 – 1 = **2**

Subtract 2 by counting back.

5 – 2 = _____

Count back from the first number.

Count out loud.

5   4   3

Stop when 2 fingers are up.

5 – 2 = **3**

1. Subtract by counting back.

9 – 1 = _____ 9, _____	10 – 2 = _____ 10, _____, _____
4 – 1 = _____ 4,	9 – 2 = _____ 9, _____, _____
6 – 1 = _____ 6, _____	7 – 2 = _____ 7, _____, _____
8 – 1 = _____ 8, _____	4 – 2 = _____ 4, _____, _____

Using a Number Line to Subtract

Use a number line to subtract.

$8 - 4 =$ __**4**__

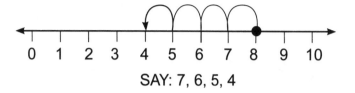

SAY: 7, 6, 5, 4

Mark a dot at 8.
Draw 4 jumps to count back.
Stop at 4.

1. Use the number line to subtract. Mark a dot to show where you start.
   Then count back by drawing the jumps. Write the answer.

$5 - 2 =$ _____

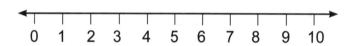

$9 - 5 =$ _____

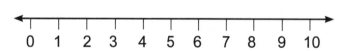

$8 - 1 =$ _____

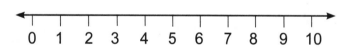

$10 - 6 =$ _____

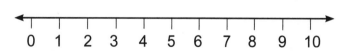

2. Use the number line to subtract. Mark a dot to show where you start. Then count back by drawing the jumps. Write the answer.

7 – 2 = _____
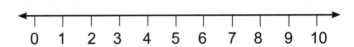

6 – 4 = _____
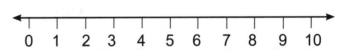

3 – 3 = _____
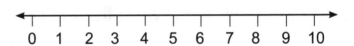

4 – 1 = _____
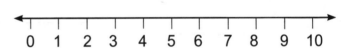

9 – 7 = _____
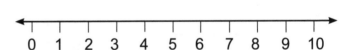

7 – 5 = _____
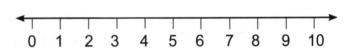

10 – 8 = _____
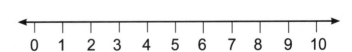

Making Subtraction Sentences

1. Cross out the blocks you want to take away. Colour the blocks left. Complete the subtraction sentence.

4 – __3__ = __1__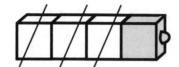

4 – ___ = ___

4 – ___ = ___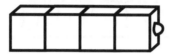

8 – ___ = ___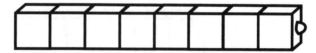

8 – ___ = ___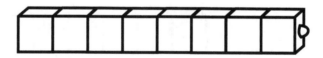

8 – ___ = ___

5 – ___ = ___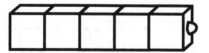

5 – ___ = ___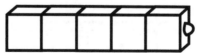

5 – ___ = ___

Making Subtraction Sentences (continued)

2. Cross out the blocks you want to take away. Colour the blocks left.
   Complete the subtraction sentence.

6 – ___ = ___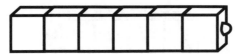

6 – ___ = ___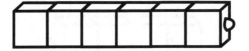

6 – ___ = ___

10 – ___ = ___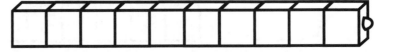

10 – ___ = ___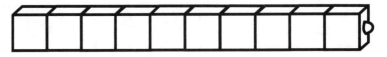

10 – ___ = ___

9 – ___ = ___

9 – ___ = ___

9 – ___ = ___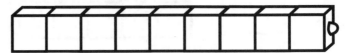

Subtraction Facts to 10

1. Draw a line from the subtraction sentences to the correct answer.

7 – 2 =

8 – 5 =

10 – 0 =

6 – 2 =

8 – 7 =

10 – 2 =

4 – 4 =

10 – 3 =

9 – 5 =

1

8

6

2

5

0

10

9

4

3

7

11 – 1 =

5 – 3 =

9 – 4 =

4 – 2 =

10 – 1 =

8 – 2 =

6 – 3 =

7 – 6 =

1 – 1 =

Story Problems

1. Solve the story problems.

There are **8** 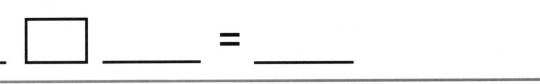 on the ground.

Then **3** go away.

How many are left?

_____ ☐ _____ = _____

There are **7** on the flower.

Then **4** fly away.

How many 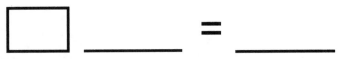 are left?

_____ ☐ _____ = _____

There are **9** on the branch.

Then **3** fly away.

How many are left?

_____ ☐ _____ = _____

Story Problems (continued)

2. Solve the story problems.

There are **6**  in the pond.

Then **2** swim away.

How many are left?

_____ ▢ _____ = _____

There are **3** under the tree.

Then **1** runs away.

How many are left?

_____ ▢ _____ = _____

There are **5**  eating cheese.

Then **4** go away.

How many are left?

_____ ▢ _____ = _____

Equal Parts

1. Circle the shape that shows two equal parts. Each part is a half.
   Colour one half.

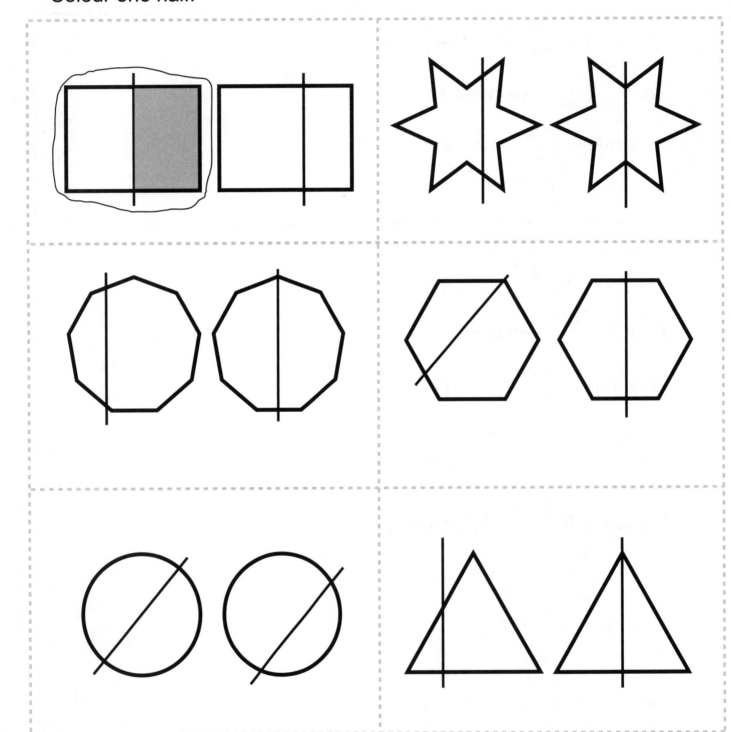

© Chalkboard Publishing

Naming the Fraction

1. What part is shaded? Circle the fraction.

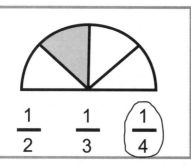

$\frac{1}{2}$ $\frac{1}{3}$ $\boxed{\frac{1}{4}}$

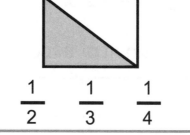

$\frac{1}{2}$ $\frac{1}{3}$ $\frac{1}{4}$

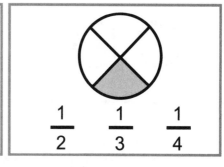

$\frac{1}{2}$ $\frac{1}{3}$ $\frac{1}{4}$

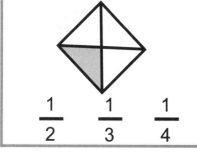

$\frac{1}{2}$ $\frac{1}{3}$ $\frac{1}{4}$

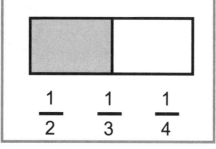

$\frac{1}{2}$ $\frac{1}{3}$ $\frac{1}{4}$

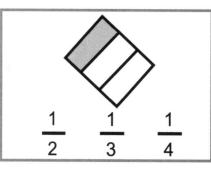

$\frac{1}{2}$ $\frac{1}{3}$ $\frac{1}{4}$

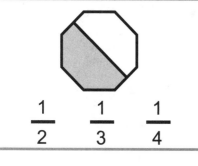

$\frac{1}{2}$ $\frac{1}{3}$ $\frac{1}{4}$

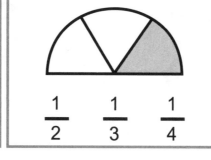

$\frac{1}{2}$ $\frac{1}{3}$ $\frac{1}{4}$

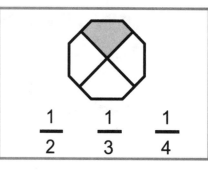

$\frac{1}{2}$ $\frac{1}{3}$ $\frac{1}{4}$

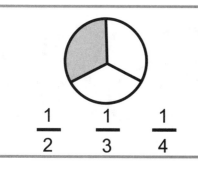

$\frac{1}{2}$ $\frac{1}{3}$ $\frac{1}{4}$

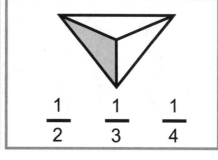

$\frac{1}{2}$ $\frac{1}{3}$ $\frac{1}{4}$

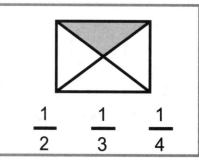

$\frac{1}{2}$ $\frac{1}{3}$ $\frac{1}{4}$

Colouring One Half

1. Colour one half of the set.

 $\frac{1}{2}$ means one part of 2 parts.

One half of the circles are coloured.

Colour $\frac{1}{2}$ green.

Colour $\frac{1}{2}$ red.

Colour $\frac{1}{2}$ blue.

Colour $\frac{1}{2}$ green.

Colour $\frac{1}{2}$ red.

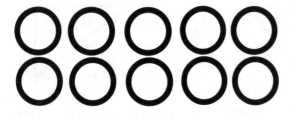

Colour $\frac{1}{2}$ blue.

Repeating Patterns

A **pattern** repeats. A pattern can be different shapes and sizes.
The **core** of the pattern are the parts that repeat over and over.

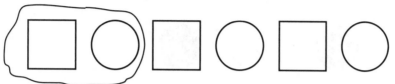

1. Circle the core of each repeating pattern. Extend the pattern.

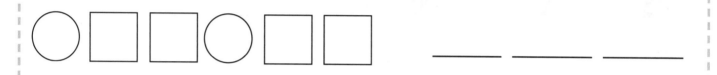

2. Circle the core of each repeating pattern. Extend the pattern.

Using Letters to Name Patterns

1. Use a letter to name each part of the pattern. Circle the core of the pattern.

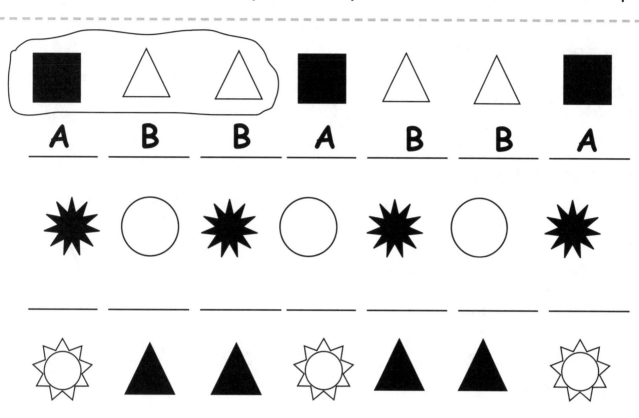

A   B   B   A   B   B   A

_____ _____ _____ _____ _____ _____ _____

_____ _____ _____ _____ _____ _____ _____

Draw your own pattern. Use a letter to name each part of the pattern.

_____ _____ _____ _____ _____

Draw your own pattern. Use a letter to name each part of the pattern.

_____ _____ _____ _____ _____

Creating Patterns

1. Create the pattern. Circle the core.

Colour an AB pattern.

Colour an AAB pattern.

Colour an ABC pattern.

Colour an ABBC pattern.

Make a pattern in which the size of the shape changes.

_____   _____   _____   _____   _____   _____

Make a pattern in which the position of the shape changes.

_____   _____   _____   _____   _____   _____

What Comes Next?

1. Make your own patterns. Use two or three colours.
   Give each pattern a name.

Name _____   _____   _____   _____

Getting to Know 2D Shapes

1. Complete.

		Connect the dots.	Draw your own.
rectangle			
circle			
triangle			
square			
pentagon			
hexagon			
rhombus			

Matching 2D Shapes

1. Draw a line from the shape to its name.

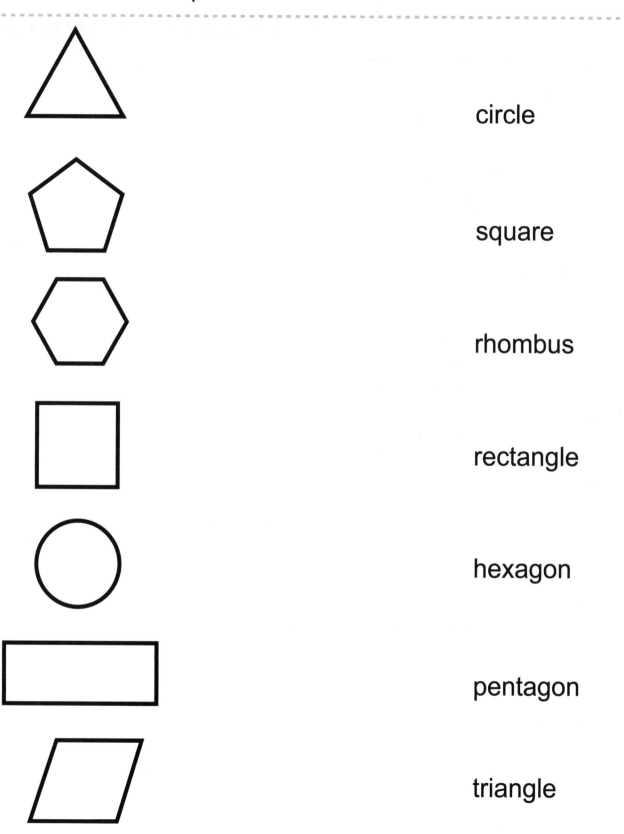

circle

square

rhombus

rectangle

hexagon

pentagon

triangle

What 2D Shapes Do You Know?

1. How many sides and corners does each shape have?

	Number of Sides	Number of Corners
rectangle		
circle		
triangle		
square		
rhombus		
pentagon		

© Chalkboard Publishing

Drawing Shapes

1. Use the shapes to draw a picture.

rectangle   rhombus   circle   triangle   square

Sorting 2D Shapes

1. Read the sorting rule. Draw the shapes that follow the rule.

Shapes with **corners.**

Shapes with **less** than **4 sides.**

Shapes with **more** than **3 sides.**

Shapes with **more** than **3 corners.**

Exploring Symmetry

A line of symmetry divides a object into 2 parts that are the exact same size and shape. Some objects have more than 1 line of symmetry. Some objects do not have a line of symmetry.

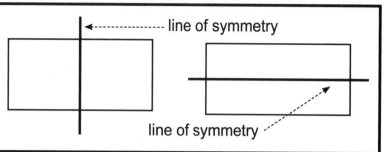

1. Draw a line of symmetry to show two sides exactly the same.

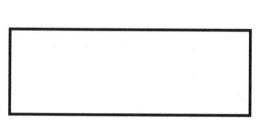

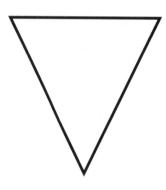

Symmetrical Shapes

1. Draw the other half of each shape.

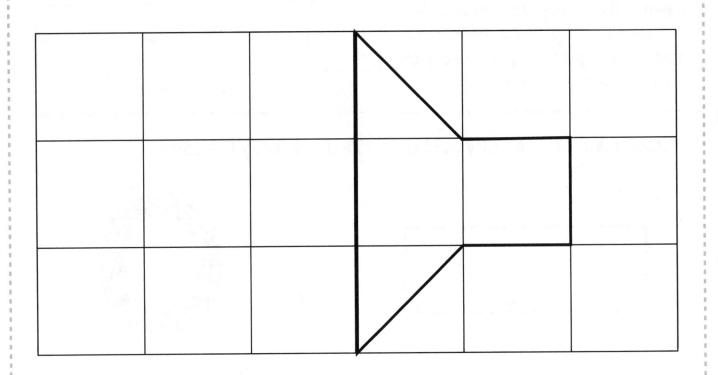

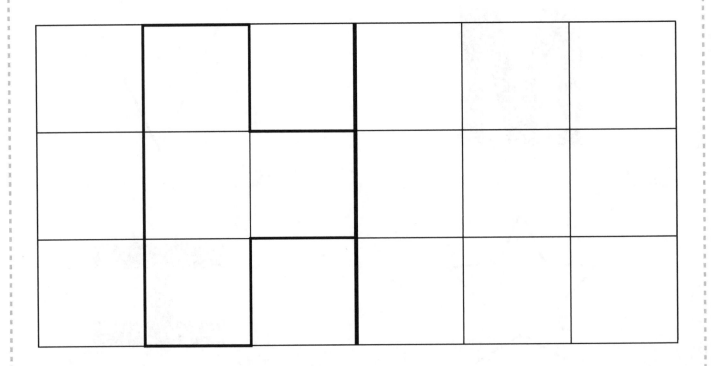

Matching 3D Objects

1. Draw a line from the 3D object to the image it looks like.

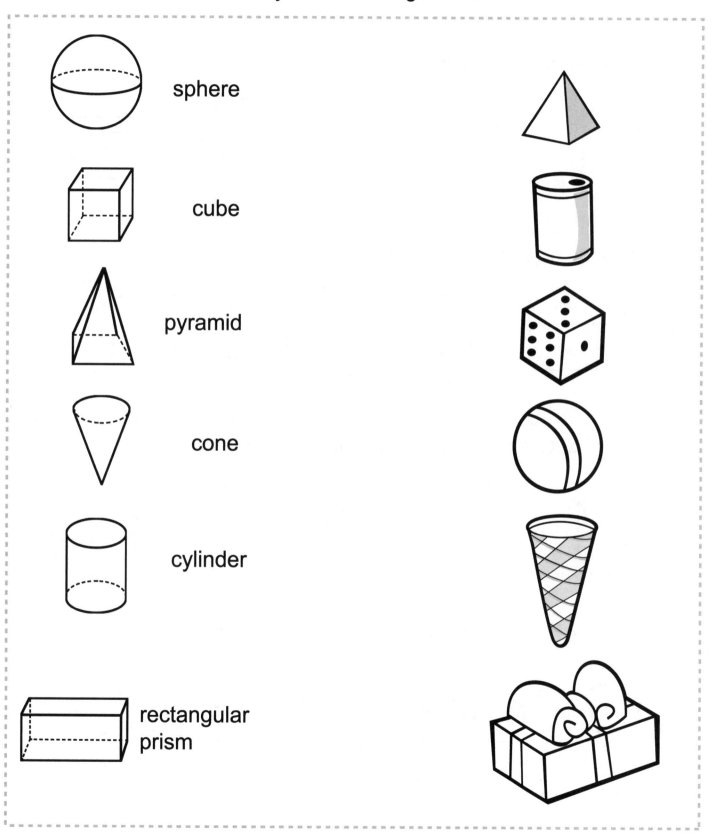

sphere

cube

pyramid

cone

cylinder

rectangular prism

Sorting 3D Objects

1. Read the rule. Circle the objects that follow the rule.

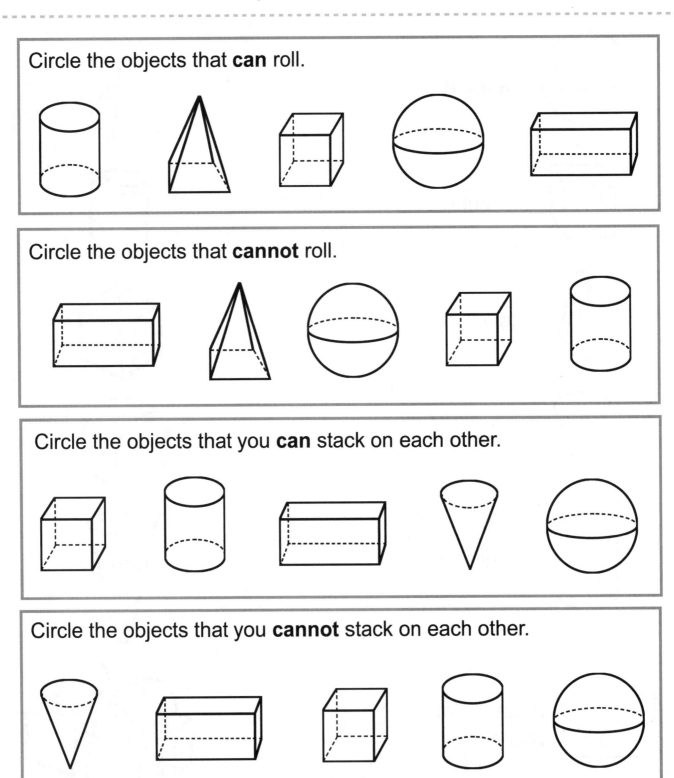

Circle the objects that **can** roll.

Circle the objects that **cannot** roll.

Circle the objects that you **can** stack on each other.

Circle the objects that you **cannot** stack on each other.

Telling Time to the Hour

A clock has an hour hand.
The hour hand is short. It shows the hour.

You can write the time in two ways. It is **5 o'clock** or **5:00**.

1. Draw a line between the times that are the same.

1 o'clock	3:00
11:00	1:00
3 o'clock	11 o'clock
5:00	5 o'clock

2. Write the time in two ways.

_____ o'clock or _____:00

_____ o'clock or _____:00

_____ o'clock or _____:00

_____ o'clock or _____:00

Telling Time to the Hour (continued)

2. Tell the time to the hour. Highlight the hour hand blue.
   Highlight the minute hand red. Hint: The minute hand is long.

____ o'clock   ____ o'clock   ____ o'clock

____ o'clock   ____ o'clock   ____ o'clock

____ o'clock   ____ o'clock   ____ o'clock

____ o'clock   ____ o'clock   ____ o'clock

Telling Time to the Half Hour

A clock has an hour hand.
The hour hand is short.
It shows the hour.

It is **3 o'clock** or **3:00**.
There are 60 minutes
in an hour.

A clock has a minute hand.
The minute hand is long. It shows
the minutes after the hour.

Count by 5s.
It is 30 minutes after 3 o'clock.
It is **half past 3** or **3:30**.

1. What time is it? Write the time two ways.

1. _____ 2. _____

1. _____ 2. _____

1. _____ 2. _____

1. _____ 2. _____

Telling Time to the Half Hour (continued)

2. Tell the time to the half hour.
   Highlight the hour hand blue. Highlight the minute hand red.

half past _____

half past _____

half past _____

half past _____

half past _____

half past _____

half past _____

half past _____

half past _____

half past _____

half past _____

half past _____

Showing the Time to the Hour

1. Draw the two hands on the clock to show the time.
   Highlight the hour hand blue. Highlight the minute hand red.

6:00

5:00

11:00

1:00

8:00

2:00

9:00

12:00

10:00

When is your bedtime?

•

•

_____

What Time Is It?

1. Circle the correct time.
   Highlight the hour hand blue. Highlight the minute hand red.

2:00 or 2:30

5:00 or 5:30

8:00 or 8:30

9:00 or 9:30

4:00 or 4:30

3:00 or 3:30

12:00 or 12:30

11:00 or 11:30

7:00 or 7:30

3:00 or 3:30

10:00 or 10:30

4:00 or 4:30

Canadian Coins

Each Canadian coin has a value.

This is a nickel.  5¢ 5 cents

(¢ means cents)

This is a dime.   10¢ 10 cents

This is a quarter.  25¢ 25 cents

This is a loonie.  100¢ 100 cents or 1 dollar

This is a toonie.  200¢ 200 cents or 2 dollars

Getting to Know Coins

1. Draw a line from the coin to its value.
   Then draw a line from the coin to its name.

100 cents toonie

25 cents loonie

5 cents  nickel

200 cents  dime

10 cents  quarter

Getting to Know Coins (continued)

2. Circle the loonies red. Circle the quarters green.
   Circle the dimes blue. Circle the nickels yellow.
   Circle the toonies orange.

BRAIN STRETCH

How many loonies? _____   How many nickels? _____

How many dimes? _____   How many quarters? _____

How many toonies? _____

Counting Nickels

_____ ¢ _____ ¢ _____ ¢ _____ ¢ = _____ ¢

_____ ¢ _____ ¢ _____ ¢ _____ ¢ _____ ¢ _____ ¢ _____ ¢ = _____ ¢

_____ ¢ _____ ¢ _____ ¢ _____ ¢ _____ ¢ _____ ¢ = _____ ¢

_____ ¢ _____ ¢ _____ ¢ _____ ¢ _____ ¢ = _____ ¢

_____ ¢ _____ ¢ _____ ¢ _____ ¢ _____ ¢ _____ ¢ _____ ¢ _____ ¢ = _____ ¢

Counting Dimes

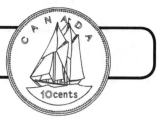

_____ ¢ _____ ¢ _____ ¢ _____ ¢ _____ ¢ = _____ ¢

_____ ¢ _____ ¢ _____ ¢ _____ ¢ _____ ¢ _____ ¢ _____ ¢ = _____ ¢

_____ ¢ _____ ¢ _____ ¢ = _____ ¢

_____ ¢ _____ ¢ _____ ¢ _____ ¢ _____ ¢ _____ ¢ _____ ¢ _____ ¢ = _____ ¢

Toy Counter

1. How much does each toy cost?

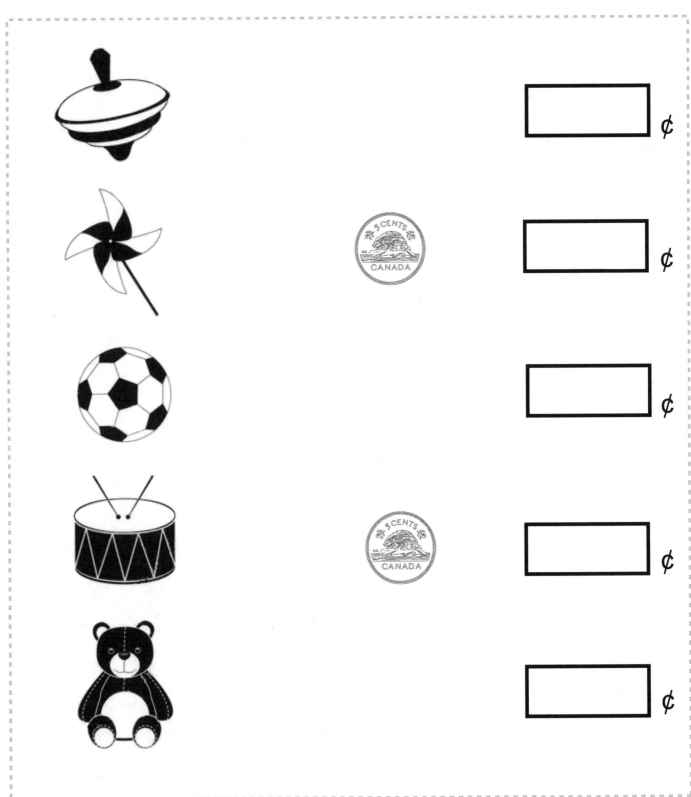

© Chalkboard Publishing

Exploring Pictographs

A pictograph uses pictures or symbols to show information or data.

Mrs. Turnbull's class made a pictograph of their favourite pet fish survey.

Each 👤 equals 1 vote. Count the number of 👤 in each row.

Fish	Number of Children Who Liked Each Fish
🐟	👤👤👤👤👤👤👤👤👤
🐟	👤👤👤👤👤👤
🐟	👤👤👤

1. How many children chose  ? _____

2. How many children chose ? _____

3. How many children chose  ? _____

4. Circle the **most** popular fish. Mark with an X the **least** popular fish.

Exploring Bar Graphs

A bar graph uses bars to show data.
This bar graph shows the favourite winter activity of children.

Read the bar graph to answer the questions.

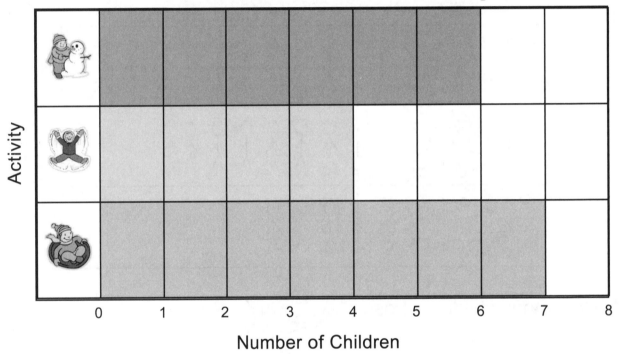

Favourite Winter Activity

Activity

Number of Children

1. How many votes? _____ _____ _____

2. Circle the **most** popular winter activity.

3. Circle the **least** popular winter activity.

Exploring Bar Graphs (continued)

Ms. Stanley's class took a survey of their favourite pets.
Count the votes for each pet and complete the bar graph.

Favourite Pet Survey

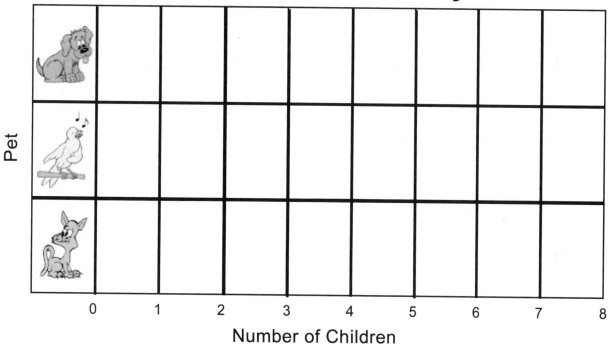

Pet

Number of Children

1. How many votes? _____  _____ _____

2. Circle the pet that 3 children chose as their favourite pet.

Exploring Tally Charts

A tally chart counts data in 1s and groups of 5.

Each single tally mark stands for 1 vote. |

Each group of five tally marks stands for 5 votes.

Ms. Yen's class made a tally chart of their favourite ice cream. Count the tally marks.

Favourite Ice Cream Flavour

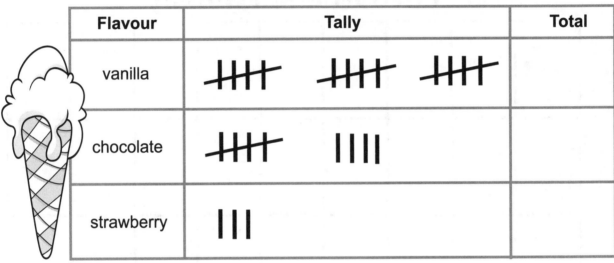

Flavour	Tally			Total
vanilla	⟍HHH	⟍HHH	⟍HHH	
chocolate	⟍HHH	||||		
strawberry	|||			

1. How many children picked vanilla? _____

2. How many children picked chocolate? _____

3. How many children picked strawberry? _____

4. Which ice cream was **most** popular? _____

5. Which ice cream was **least** popular? _____

Shortest to Tallest

1. Number the creatures in order from shortest to tallest. Use 1, 2, and 3.

Tallest to Shortest

1. Number the animals in order from tallest to shortest. Use 1, 2, and 3.

© Chalkboard Publishing

Exploring Measuring

1. Count the feet to measure the creatures. About how long is each creature?

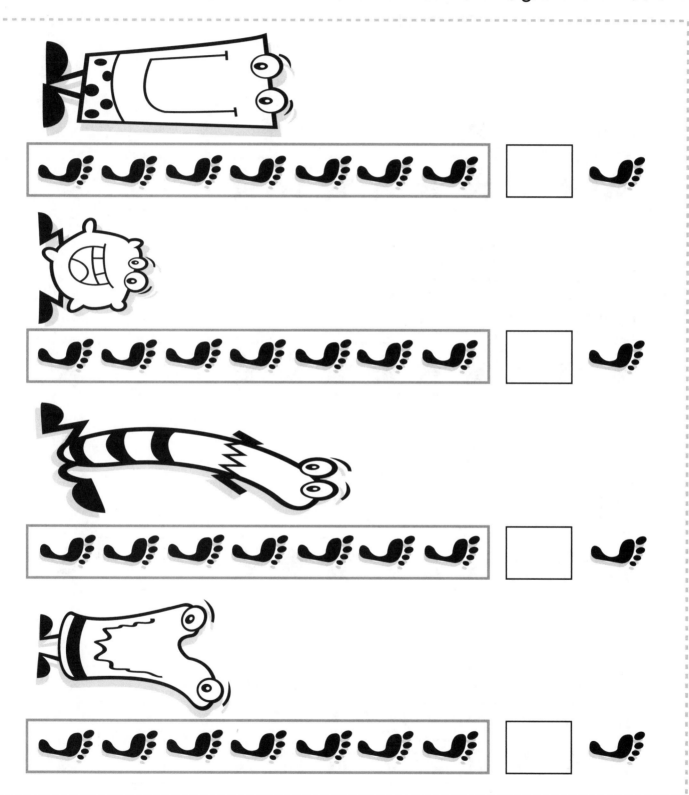

Exploring Measuring (continued)

2. Count the stars to measure the pencils.
   About how long is each pencil?

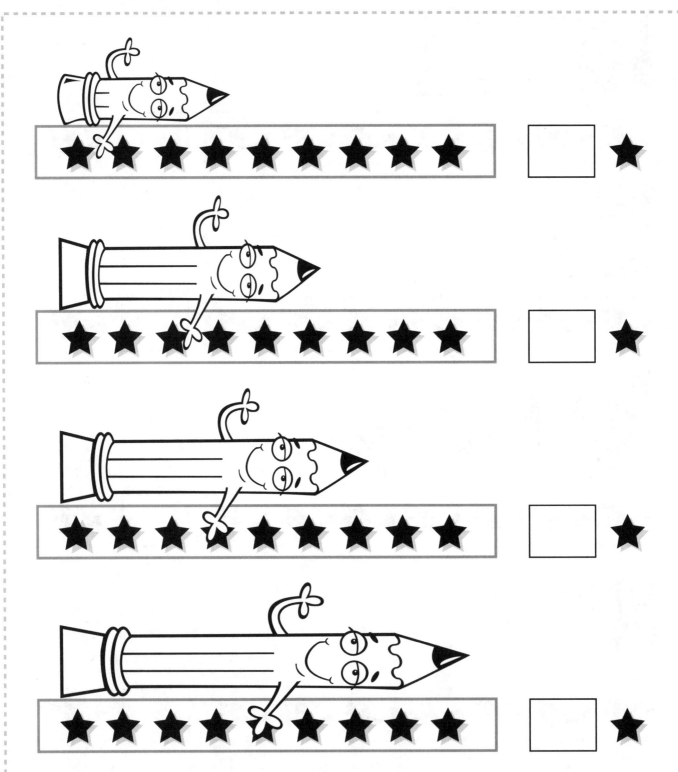

© Chalkboard Publishing

Exploring Measuring (continued)

3. How many centimetres long is each pencil?

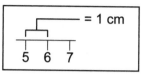

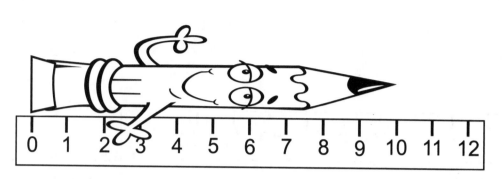

 centimetres

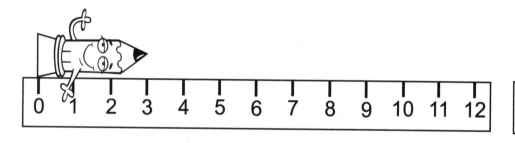

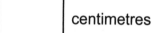 centimetres

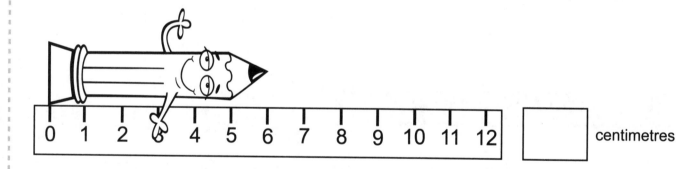

centimetres

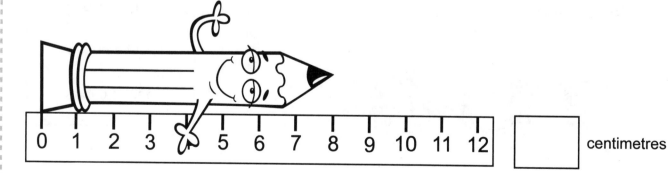

centimetres

Exploring Measuring (continued)

4. Find an object and then measure in centimetres.

0 1 2 3 4 5 6 7 8 9 10 11 12

centimetres

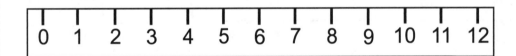

0 1 2 3 4 5 6 7 8 9 10 11 12

centimetres

BRAIN STRETCH

About how many cubes long is the caterpillar?
Circle the answer.

about **3** cubes

about **5** cubes

about **7** cubes

Exploring Mass

Mass measures how much something weighs.

1. What is the mass of the creature? Count the blocks to find out.

_____ blocks

_____ blocks

_____ blocks

_____ blocks

Exploring Mass (continued)

2. Some blocks are missing. Draw blocks to make the same mass on both sides.

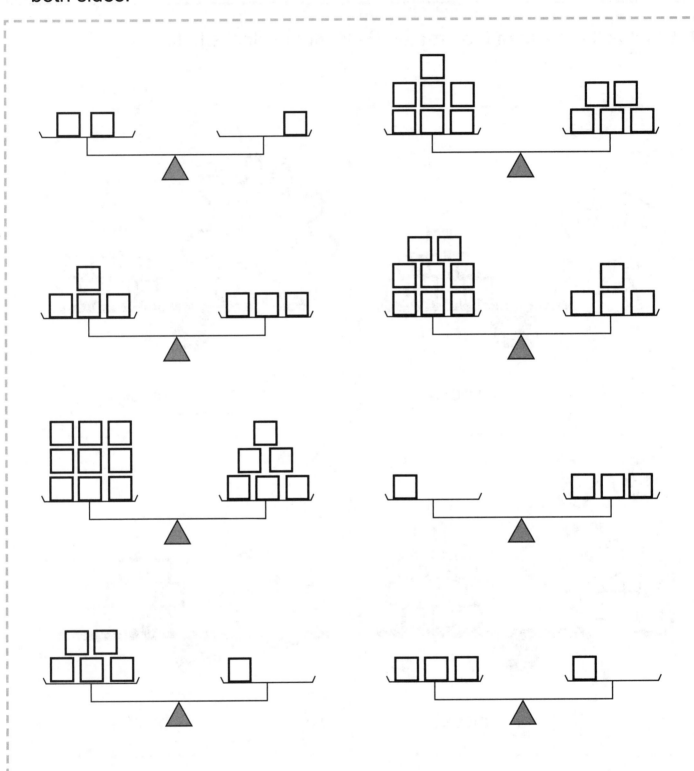

© Chalkboard Publishing

Addition Doubles

1. Write the number sentence.

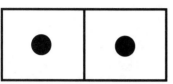

_____ + _____ = _____

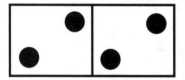

_____ + _____ = _____

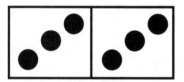

_____ + _____ = _____

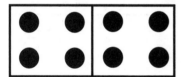

_____ + _____ = _____

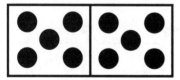

_____ + _____ = _____

_____ + _____ = _____

Addition Doubles Plus 1

1. Use doubles plus 1 to add.

If   6 + 6 = **12**

Then   6 + 7 = **13**

If   1 + 1 = _____

Then _____ + _____ = _____

If   9 + 9 = _____

Then _____ + _____ = _____

If   5 + 5 = _____

Then _____ + _____ = _____

If   8 + 8 = _____

Then _____ + _____ = _____

If   10 + 10 = _____

Then _____ + _____ = _____

If   3 + 3 = _____

Then _____ + _____ = _____

If   2 + 2 = _____

Then _____ + _____ = _____

If   7 + 7 = _____

Then _____ + _____ = _____

If   4 + 4 = _____

Then _____ + _____ = _____

Adding by Making 10

1. Make a group of 10 to help you add.

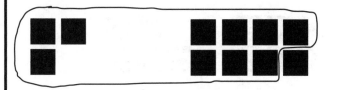

3 + 8 = 10 + <u>1</u> = <u>11</u>

Circle 10. There is 1 more block. Use 10 to add.

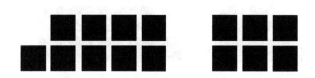

9 + 6 = 10 + ___ = ___

 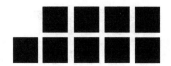

4 + 9 = 10 + ___ = ___

7 + 7 = 10 + ___ = ___

5 + 7 = 10 + ___ = ___

5 + 8 = 10 + ___ = ___

2. Make a group of 10 to help you add.

5 + 9 = 10 + ___ = ___

6 + 5 = 10 + ___ = ___

8 + 7 = 10 + ___ = ___

9 + 7 = 10 + ___ = ___

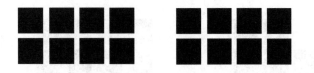

8 + 8 = 10 + ___ = ___

9 + 9 = 10 + ___ = ___

3. Make a group of 10 to help you add.

8 + 6 = 10 + ___ = ___

7 + 8 = 10 + ___ = ___

6 + 9 = 10 + ___ = ___

9 + 8 = 10 + ___ = ___

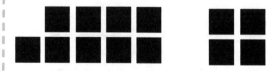

9 + 4 = 10 + ___ = ___

2 + 9 = 10 + ___ = ___

Addition Practice—Sums from 11 to 15

1. Add. Use the number line or counters to help you add.
   Hint: Start with the greater number.

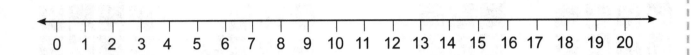

8 + 6	9 + 3	10 + 5	9 + 6	14 + 3
5 + 6	10 + 5	11 + 3	8 + 4	7 + 7
10 + 3	6 + 6	13 + 1	9 + 4	7 + 6
9 + 5	5 + 7	9 + 2	8 + 5	10 + 2

Addition Practice—Sums from 16 to 20

1. Use the number line or counters to help you add.

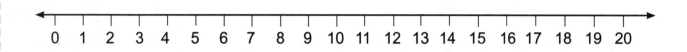

$$9 + 8$$

$$6 + 10$$

$$16 + 2$$

$$8 + 8$$

$$10 + 7$$

$$17 + 2$$

$$16 + 0$$

$$14 + 6$$

$$12 + 5$$

$$14 + 2$$

$$8 + 10$$

$$12 + 4$$

$$9 + 10$$

$$18 + 2$$

$$9 + 9$$

$$11 + 6$$

$$11 + 8$$

$$7 + 9$$

$$15 + 3$$

$$10 + 10$$

Math Riddle: Addition Facts to 20

What kind of socks do bears wear?

___ ___ ___ ___ | ___ ___ ___ ___ ___ ___ |
13 10 16   8 | 20 11 16   9   16 11 |

___ ___ ___ ___ ___ | ___ ___ ___ ___ | ___ ___ ___ ___ !
13 10 16 17 11 | 6 16 13 11 | 9 16 16 13

A	B	C	E
6 + 7 = ____	2 + 4 = ____	7 + 5 = ____	8 + 8 = ____
F	**H**	**I**	**L**
4 + 5 = ____	5 + 5 = ____	10 + 7 = ____	8 + 7 = ____
M	**P**	**Q**	**R**
3 + 4 = ____	19 + 1 = ____	9 + 9 = ____	5 + 6 = ____
S	**T**	**W**	**Y**
7 + 7 = ____	6 + 7 = ____	1 + 4 = ____	3 + 5 = ____

Using a Number Line to Subtract

Subtract using a number line.

$12 - 3 =$ **9**

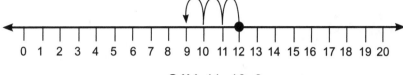

SAY: 11, 10, 9

Mark a dot at 12.
Draw 3 steps to count back.
Stop at 9.

1. Use the number line to subtract. Mark a dot to show where you start.
   Then count back by drawing the steps. Write the answer.

$15 - 1 =$ _____

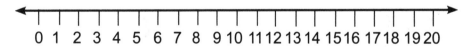

$19 - 4 =$ _____

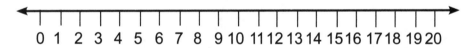

$13 - 3 =$ _____

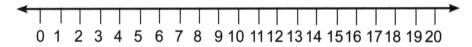

$17 - 6 =$ _____

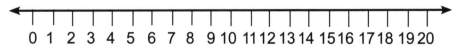

Subtraction Match

1. Draw a line from the number sentence to the correct answer.

12 – 3	1	11 – 3
16 – 8	2	18 – 9
10 – 5	3	9 – 8
6 – 3	4	12 – 9
17 – 10	5	13 – 6
20 – 10	6	7 – 5
8 – 4	7	14 – 7
11 – 9	8	8 – 3
13 – 7	**9**	10 – 0
5 – 4	10	13 – 9

© Chalkboard Publishing

Subtracting 1 or 2 by Counting Back

1. Count back to subtract.

14 – 1 = __13__ 14, __13__	19 – 2 = __17__ 19, __18__, __17__
17 – 1 = _____ 17, _____	18 – 2 = _____ 18, _____, _____
16 – 1 = _____ 16, _____	20 – 2 = _____ 20, _____, _____
15 – 1 = _____ 15, _____	14 – 2 = _____ 14, _____, _____
19 – 1 = _____ 19, _____	13 – 2 = _____ 13, _____, _____
13 – 1 = _____ 13, _____	16 – 2 = _____ 16, _____, _____
20 – 1 = _____ 20, _____	15 – 2 = _____ 15, _____, _____

Making 10 to Subtract

1. Make 10 to make an easier problem. Then subtract.

$12 - 9 =$

$12 - 9 = \underline{\textbf{13}} - 10 = \underline{\textbf{3}}$

I know 9 + 1 = 10.
So, I add 1 to each number.
Then I subtract to get the answer.

$19 - 6 =$

$19 - 6 = \underline{\quad} - 10 = \underline{\quad}$

Add 4 to each number.

$15 - 7 =$

$15 - 7 = \underline{\quad} - 10 = \underline{\quad}$

Add ___ to each number.

$14 - 8 =$

$14 - 8 = \underline{\quad} - 10 = \underline{\quad}$

Add ___ to each number.

$18 - 7 =$

$18 - 7 = \underline{\quad} - 10 = \underline{\quad}$

Add ___ to each number.

$13 - 9 =$

$13 - 9 = \underline{\quad} - 10 = \underline{\quad}$

Add ___ to each number.

$17 - 6 =$

$17 - 6 = \underline{\quad} - 10 = \underline{\quad}$

Add ___ to each number.

$16 - 7 =$

$16 - 7 = \underline{\quad} - 10 = \underline{\quad}$

Add ___ to each number.

Subtracting by 7, 8, or 9 from 11 to 20

1. Find each difference. You can subtract by counting back or use counters to help.

14 − 9	11 − 7	14 − 8	16 − 9	10 − 9
15 − 8	12 − 7	18 − 8	13 − 9	16 − 7
12 − 9	19 − 9	16 − 8	14 − 7	11 − 9
15 − 7	13 − 8	17 − 9	19 − 8	20 − 8
17 − 7	11 − 8	15 − 9	20 − 7	12 − 8

Subtraction Practice: Differences from 11 to 15

1. Find each difference. You can subtract by counting back.

15 − 9	11 − 7	13 − 7	12 − 8	14 − 2

12 − 3	14 − 4	12 − 9	15 − 0	11 − 6

12 − 5	14 − 6	15 − 4	11 − 4	13 − 2

15 − 6	11 − 5	14 − 7	12 − 4	13 − 1

BRAIN STRETCH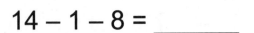

$14 - 1 - 8 =$ _____ $19 - 9 - 1 =$ _____

$15 - 4 - 6 =$ _____ $20 - 3 - 8 =$ _____

Subtraction Practice: Differences from 16 to 20

1. Find each difference. You can subtract by counting back.

17 − 9	18 − 8	20 − 10	16 − 7	19 − 9
16 − 9	20 − 3	18 − 9	17 − 7	19 − 10
17 − 10	16 − 3	20 − 1	18 − 2	19 − 1
18 − 2	19 − 2	16 − 8	17 − 1	20 − 2
17 − 8	19 − 0	20 − 5	18 − 6	16 − 5

Subtraction Practice: Differences from 11 to 20

1. Find each difference. You can subtract by counting back.

17 − 10	19 − 9	16 − 2	18 − 9	15 − 10
15 − 2	11 − 8	20 − 2	14 − 7	11 − 9
14 − 6	12 − 2	13 − 5	16 − 10	15 − 8
13 − 6	12 − 8	14 − 9	20 − 10	11 − 5

BRAIN STRETCH

17 − 6 − 5 = _____   19 − 2 − 2 = _____

15 − 1 − 9 = _____   20 − 8 − 7 = _____

Math Riddle: Subtraction Facts to 20

What is a shark's favourite sandwich?

___ ___ ___ ___ ___ ___ | ___ ___ ___ ___ ___ ___ |
13   6   16   15   1   18   11   1   18   18   6   17

___ ___ ___ | ___ ___ ___ ___ ___ ___ ___ ___ ___ !
16   15   12   3   6   7   7   8   10   14   4   9

A	B	D	E
19 – 3 = ____	12 – 1 = ____	13 – 1 = ____	12 – 6 = ____
F	**H**	**I**	**J**
15 – 5 = ____	11 – 2 = ____	16 – 2 = ____	11 – 8 = ____
L	**N**	**P**	**R**
9 – 2 = ____	17 – 2 = ____	16 – 3 = ____	17 – 0 = ____
S	**T**	**U**	**Y**
8 – 4 = ____	20 – 2 = ____	10 – 9 = ____	10 – 2 = ____

How to Use the Addition Table

The numbers in the dark border down the side show the rows. The numbers in the dark border at the top show the columns. You can use this table to add to find the sum of two numbers.
For example, find the sum of 6 + 5.

First way: Go down to the 6 row. Put your finger on the 6. Then slide your finger along the 6 row to the 5 column. The number in the square is your answer! So, 6 + 5 = 11.

Second way: Go down to the 5 row. Then slide your finger along the 5 row to the 6 column to get your answer.

Third way: Go to the 6 column. Then slide your finger down to the 5 row to get your answer.

+	0	1	2	3	4	5	6	7	8	9	10
0	0	1	2	3	4	5	6	7	8	9	10
1	1	2	3	4	5	6	7	8	9	10	11
2	2	3	4	5	6	7	8	9	10	11	12
3	3	4	5	6	7	8	9	10	11	12	13
4	4	5	6	7	8	9	10	11	12	13	14
5	5	6	7	8	9	10	11	12	13	14	15
6	6	7	8	9	10	11	12	13	14	15	16
7	7	8	9	10	11	12	13	14	15	16	17
8	8	9	10	11	12	13	14	15	16	17	18
9	9	10	11	12	13	14	15	16	17	18	19
10	10	11	12	13	14	15	16	17	18	19	20

Addition Test 1—Sums to 1, 2, 3, 4, and 5

$$\begin{array}{r} 2 \\ +\ 1 \\ \hline \end{array} \qquad \begin{array}{r} 2 \\ +\ 0 \\ \hline \end{array} \qquad \begin{array}{r} 0 \\ +\ 5 \\ \hline \end{array} \qquad \begin{array}{r} 3 \\ +\ 1 \\ \hline \end{array} \qquad \begin{array}{r} 1 \\ +\ 0 \\ \hline \end{array} \qquad \begin{array}{r} 4 \\ +\ 1 \\ \hline \end{array} \qquad \begin{array}{r} 1 \\ +\ 2 \\ \hline \end{array}$$

$$\begin{array}{r} 5 \\ +\ 0 \\ \hline \end{array} \qquad \begin{array}{r} 3 \\ +\ 2 \\ \hline \end{array} \qquad \begin{array}{r} 0 \\ +\ 1 \\ \hline \end{array} \qquad \begin{array}{r} 3 \\ +\ 0 \\ \hline \end{array} \qquad \begin{array}{r} 2 \\ +\ 2 \\ \hline \end{array} \qquad \begin{array}{r} 0 \\ +\ 3 \\ \hline \end{array} \qquad \begin{array}{r} 4 \\ +\ 0 \\ \hline \end{array}$$

$$\begin{array}{r} 1 \\ +\ 1 \\ \hline \end{array} \qquad \begin{array}{r} 1 \\ +\ 3 \\ \hline \end{array} \qquad \begin{array}{r} 0 \\ +\ 2 \\ \hline \end{array} \qquad \begin{array}{r} 1 \\ +\ 4 \\ \hline \end{array} \qquad \begin{array}{r} 2 \\ +\ 3 \\ \hline \end{array} \qquad \begin{array}{r} 0 \\ +\ 4 \\ \hline \end{array}$$

Number Correct

$$\frac{}{20}$$

Addition Test 2—Sums to 1, 2, 3, 4, and 5

$$\begin{array}{r} 1 \\ +\ 2 \\ \hline \end{array} \qquad \begin{array}{r} 2 \\ +\ 3 \\ \hline \end{array} \qquad \begin{array}{r} 0 \\ +\ 3 \\ \hline \end{array} \qquad \begin{array}{r} 2 \\ +\ 0 \\ \hline \end{array} \qquad \begin{array}{r} 3 \\ +\ 2 \\ \hline \end{array} \qquad \begin{array}{r} 0 \\ +\ 2 \\ \hline \end{array} \qquad \begin{array}{r} 1 \\ +\ 1 \\ \hline \end{array}$$

$$\begin{array}{r} 4 \\ +\ 0 \\ \hline \end{array} \qquad \begin{array}{r} 3 \\ +\ 1 \\ \hline \end{array} \qquad \begin{array}{r} 5 \\ +\ 0 \\ \hline \end{array} \qquad \begin{array}{r} 2 \\ +\ 2 \\ \hline \end{array} \qquad \begin{array}{r} 0 \\ +\ 4 \\ \hline \end{array} \qquad \begin{array}{r} 4 \\ +\ 1 \\ \hline \end{array} \qquad \begin{array}{r} 1 \\ +\ 3 \\ \hline \end{array}$$

$$\begin{array}{r} 0 \\ +\ 1 \\ \hline \end{array} \qquad \begin{array}{r} 3 \\ +\ 0 \\ \hline \end{array} \qquad \begin{array}{r} 2 \\ +\ 1 \\ \hline \end{array} \qquad \begin{array}{r} 1 \\ +\ 0 \\ \hline \end{array} \qquad \begin{array}{r} 1 \\ +\ 4 \\ \hline \end{array} \qquad \begin{array}{r} 0 \\ +\ 5 \\ \hline \end{array}$$

Number Correct

$$\frac{}{20}$$

Addition Test 3—Sums to 1, 2, 3, 4, and 5

2 + 2	3 + 0	0 + 5	3 + 2	1 + 0	4 + 1	1 + 2
5 + 0	0 + 2	1 + 3	2 + 1	1 + 4	0 + 3	4 + 0
1 + 1	3 + 1	2 + 0	2 + 3	0 + 1	0 + 4	

Number Correct

_____
20

Addition Test 4—Sums to 1, 2, 3, 4, and 5

1 + 2	2 + 3	0 + 3	2 + 0	3 + 2	0 + 2	1 + 1
0 + 5	1 + 0	2 + 2	5 + 0	0 + 3	4 + 0	1 + 3
0 + 1	2 + 1	3 + 0	1 + 4	0 + 4	4 + 1	

Number Correct

_____
20

Addition Test 5—Sums to 1, 2, 3, 4, and 5

3 + 0	5 + 0	4 + 1	0 + 5	1 + 0	2 + 3	0 + 1
0 + 4	3 + 2	0 + 3	1 + 2	2 + 1	4 + 0	3 + 1
2 + 2	1 + 4	0 + 2	1 + 3	2 + 0	1 + 1	Number Correct ――― 20

Addition Test 6—Sums to 1, 2, 3, 4, and 5

3 + 2	1 + 3	0 + 3	5 + 0	2 + 2	0 + 2	4 + 1
3 + 1	1 + 0	2 + 3	1 + 2	1 + 4	4 + 0	1 + 3
0 + 1	2 + 1	2 + 0	3 + 0	0 + 4	0 + 5	Number Correct ――― 20

Addition Test 7—Sums to 1, 2, 3, 4, and 5

1 + 1	5 + 0	2 + 3	2 + 2	0 + 2	2 + 1	4 + 0
2 + 0	3 + 2	0 + 4	0 + 5	1 + 0	3 + 1	4 + 1
1 + 2	0 + 1	1 + 3	1 + 4	0 + 3	3 + 0	Number Correct

_____
20

Addition Test 8—Sums to 1, 2, 3, 4, and 5

1 + 2	2 + 3	1 + 1	2 + 0	3 + 2	0 + 2	3 + 0
0 + 4	2 + 1	2 + 2	5 + 0	0 + 3	4 + 1	1 + 3
0 + 1	0 + 5	3 + 1	1 + 0	1 + 4	4 + 0	Number Correct

_____
20

Addition Test 9—Sums to 1, 2, 3, 4, and 5

4	2	0	4	1	0	2
+ 1	+ 3	+ 5	+ 0	+ 0	+ 4	+ 2

5	1	0	3	3	0	2
+ 0	+ 2	+ 1	+ 2	+ 1	+ 3	+ 0

2	1	0	1	3	1
+ 1	+ 3	+ 2	+ 4	+ 0	+ 1

Number Correct

—— 20

Addition Test 10—Sums to 1, 2, 3, 4, and 5

1	2	5	2	3	0	1
+ 2	+ 3	+ 0	+ 2	+ 2	+ 2	+ 1

4	1	2	0	0	4	1
+ 0	+ 0	+ 1	+ 5	+ 3	+ 1	+ 3

0	3	0	2	1	3
+ 1	+ 1	+ 4	+ 0	+ 4	+ 0

Number Correct

—— 20

Addition Test 1—Sums to 6, 7, 8, 9, and 10

5 + 1	8 + 2	7 + 2	3 + 5	9 + 0	5 + 2	3 + 3
2 + 8	10 + 0	6 + 1	4 + 4	1 + 8	4 + 2	3 + 6
5 + 5	6 + 2	3 + 7	7 + 1	1 + 9	2 + 4	Number Correct _____ 20

Addition Test 2—Sums to 6, 7, 8, 9, and 10

8 + 1	2 + 7	7 + 3	1 + 6	5 + 4	2 + 8	3 + 3
10 + 0	3 + 6	6 + 0	3 + 4	1 + 5	8 + 0	6 + 3
1 + 9	4 + 4	8 + 2	3 + 5	5 + 2	7 + 1	Number Correct _____ 20

Addition Test 3—Sums to 6, 7, 8, 9, and 10

2 + 5	6 + 4	7 + 3	3 + 3	4 + 2	8 + 1	4 + 3
5 + 4	3 + 5	8 + 2	2 + 4	5 + 2	3 + 7	6 + 2
1 + 9	0 + 7	10 + 0	5 + 5	6 + 3	2 + 8	Number Correct —— 20

Addition Test 4—Sums to 6, 7, 8, 9, and 10

3 + 5	2 + 8	7 + 0	3 + 3	4 + 6	5 + 2	5 + 4
9 + 1	0 + 9	3 + 4	2 + 4	7 + 3	1 + 5	8 + 2
6 + 1	2 + 6	6 + 3	5 + 1	5 + 5	7 + 1	Number Correct —— 20

Addition Test 5—Sums to 6, 7, 8, 9, and 10

$$\begin{array}{c}6\\+\ 3\\\hline\end{array}\qquad\begin{array}{c}8\\+\ 2\\\hline\end{array}\qquad\begin{array}{c}1\\+\ 5\\\hline\end{array}\qquad\begin{array}{c}3\\+\ 6\\\hline\end{array}\qquad\begin{array}{c}2\\+\ 5\\\hline\end{array}\qquad\begin{array}{c}5\\+\ 5\\\hline\end{array}\qquad\begin{array}{c}2\\+\ 6\\\hline\end{array}$$

$$\begin{array}{c}5\\+\ 2\\\hline\end{array}\qquad\begin{array}{c}10\\+\ 0\\\hline\end{array}\qquad\begin{array}{c}1\\+\ 7\\\hline\end{array}\qquad\begin{array}{c}2\\+\ 7\\\hline\end{array}\qquad\begin{array}{c}1\\+\ 9\\\hline\end{array}\qquad\begin{array}{c}0\\+\ 6\\\hline\end{array}\qquad\begin{array}{c}3\\+\ 5\\\hline\end{array}$$

$$\begin{array}{c}3\\+\ 4\\\hline\end{array}\qquad\begin{array}{c}4\\+\ 4\\\hline\end{array}\qquad\begin{array}{c}7\\+\ 3\\\hline\end{array}\qquad\begin{array}{c}0\\+\ 9\\\hline\end{array}\qquad\begin{array}{c}3\\+\ 3\\\hline\end{array}\qquad\begin{array}{c}4\\+\ 2\\\hline\end{array}$$

Number Correct

———
20

Addition Test 6—Sums to 6, 7, 8, 9, and 10

$$\begin{array}{c}4\\+\ 2\\\hline\end{array}\qquad\begin{array}{c}1\\+\ 6\\\hline\end{array}\qquad\begin{array}{c}0\\+\ 8\\\hline\end{array}\qquad\begin{array}{c}1\\+\ 7\\\hline\end{array}\qquad\begin{array}{c}7\\+\ 3\\\hline\end{array}\qquad\begin{array}{c}3\\+\ 5\\\hline\end{array}\qquad\begin{array}{c}10\\+\ 0\\\hline\end{array}$$

$$\begin{array}{c}3\\+\ 4\\\hline\end{array}\qquad\begin{array}{c}7\\+\ 2\\\hline\end{array}\qquad\begin{array}{c}6\\+\ 3\\\hline\end{array}\qquad\begin{array}{c}0\\+\ 9\\\hline\end{array}\qquad\begin{array}{c}5\\+\ 1\\\hline\end{array}\qquad\begin{array}{c}4\\+\ 6\\\hline\end{array}\qquad\begin{array}{c}2\\+\ 5\\\hline\end{array}$$

$$\begin{array}{c}6\\+\ 0\\\hline\end{array}\qquad\begin{array}{c}5\\+\ 5\\\hline\end{array}\qquad\begin{array}{c}4\\+\ 4\\\hline\end{array}\qquad\begin{array}{c}8\\+\ 2\\\hline\end{array}\qquad\begin{array}{c}3\\+\ 3\\\hline\end{array}\qquad\begin{array}{c}1\\+\ 9\\\hline\end{array}$$

Number Correct

———
20

Addition Test 7—Sums to 6, 7, 8, 9, and 10

$$
\begin{array}{ccccccc}
1 & 5 & 2 & 7 & 8 & 6 & 4 \\
+\,5 & +\,3 & +\,4 & +\,2 & +\,0 & +\,1 & +\,6 \\
\end{array}
$$

$$
\begin{array}{ccccccc}
5 & 1 & 8 & 4 & 1 & 5 & 0 \\
+\,2 & +\,9 & +\,2 & +\,3 & +\,7 & +\,4 & +\,8 \\
\end{array}
$$

$$
\begin{array}{cccccc}
3 & 7 & 6 & 5 & 4 & 10 \\
+\,3 & +\,0 & +\,3 & +\,5 & +\,2 & +\,0 \\
\end{array}
$$

Number Correct

―――
20

Addition Test 8—Sums to 6, 7, 8, 9, and 10

$$
\begin{array}{ccccccc}
4 & 3 & 5 & 1 & 3 & 9 & 6 \\
+\,6 & +\,5 & +\,1 & +\,8 & +\,4 & +\,1 & +\,0 \\
\end{array}
$$

$$
\begin{array}{ccccccc}
8 & 2 & 10 & 6 & 4 & 5 & 6 \\
+\,0 & +\,4 & +\,0 & +\,0 & +\,4 & +\,2 & +\,3 \\
\end{array}
$$

$$
\begin{array}{cccccc}
1 & 4 & 6 & 3 & 9 & 1 \\
+\,7 & +\,5 & +\,4 & +\,3 & +\,1 & +\,6 \\
\end{array}
$$

Number Correct

―――
20

Addition Test 9—Sums to 6, 7, 8, 9, and 10

$$\begin{array}{c}3\\+5\\\hline\end{array}\qquad\begin{array}{c}5\\+2\\\hline\end{array}\qquad\begin{array}{c}10\\+0\\\hline\end{array}\qquad\begin{array}{c}6\\+3\\\hline\end{array}\qquad\begin{array}{c}4\\+4\\\hline\end{array}\qquad\begin{array}{c}2\\+4\\\hline\end{array}\qquad\begin{array}{c}1\\+9\\\hline\end{array}$$

$$\begin{array}{c}7\\+0\\\hline\end{array}\qquad\begin{array}{c}3\\+3\\\hline\end{array}\qquad\begin{array}{c}6\\+4\\\hline\end{array}\qquad\begin{array}{c}1\\+7\\\hline\end{array}\qquad\begin{array}{c}8\\+2\\\hline\end{array}\qquad\begin{array}{c}0\\+9\\\hline\end{array}\qquad\begin{array}{c}6\\+1\\\hline\end{array}$$

$$\begin{array}{c}8\\+1\\\hline\end{array}\qquad\begin{array}{c}4\\+2\\\hline\end{array}\qquad\begin{array}{c}3\\+7\\\hline\end{array}\qquad\begin{array}{c}2\\+6\\\hline\end{array}\qquad\begin{array}{c}3\\+4\\\hline\end{array}\qquad\begin{array}{c}4\\+5\\\hline\end{array}$$

Number Correct

____
20

Addition Test 10—Sums to 6, 7, 8, 9, and 10

$$\begin{array}{c}1\\+6\\\hline\end{array}\qquad\begin{array}{c}2\\+8\\\hline\end{array}\qquad\begin{array}{c}1\\+5\\\hline\end{array}\qquad\begin{array}{c}5\\+4\\\hline\end{array}\qquad\begin{array}{c}3\\+3\\\hline\end{array}\qquad\begin{array}{c}4\\+6\\\hline\end{array}\qquad\begin{array}{c}5\\+2\\\hline\end{array}$$

$$\begin{array}{c}7\\+2\\\hline\end{array}\qquad\begin{array}{c}3\\+4\\\hline\end{array}\qquad\begin{array}{c}8\\+2\\\hline\end{array}\qquad\begin{array}{c}5\\+3\\\hline\end{array}\qquad\begin{array}{c}4\\+5\\\hline\end{array}\qquad\begin{array}{c}2\\+4\\\hline\end{array}\qquad\begin{array}{c}6\\+3\\\hline\end{array}$$

$$\begin{array}{c}0\\+7\\\hline\end{array}\qquad\begin{array}{c}8\\+1\\\hline\end{array}\qquad\begin{array}{c}10\\+0\\\hline\end{array}\qquad\begin{array}{c}4\\+4\\\hline\end{array}\qquad\begin{array}{c}2\\+6\\\hline\end{array}\qquad\begin{array}{c}1\\+7\\\hline\end{array}$$

Number Correct

____
20

Addition Test 1—Sums to 11, 12, 13, 14, and 15

8 + 4	6 + 7	12 + 2	14 + 1	3 + 8	15 + 0	10 + 3
5 + 8	9 + 5	7 + 6	4 + 7	2 + 9	6 + 6	9 + 4
13 + 2	1 + 12	6 + 8	8 + 5	6 + 6	8 + 7	

Number Correct

_____
20

Addition Test 2—Sums to 11, 12, 13, 14, and 15

3 + 9	5 + 6	7 + 4	6 + 8	9 + 6	8 + 4	7 + 5
5 + 8	7 + 7	8 + 6	7 + 8	12 + 1	6 + 6	9 + 5
6 + 7	12 + 3	6 + 5	4 + 8	13 + 2	9 + 4	

Number Correct

_____
20

Addition Test 3—Sums to 11, 12, 13, 14, and 15

6	11	9	13	8	7	9
+ 9	+ 2	+ 3	+ 1	+ 4	+ 6	+ 4

12	14	8	7	1	10	10
+ 0	+ 1	+ 5	+ 7	+ 13	+ 3	+ 5

6	8	7	3	12	5
+ 5	+ 6	+ 8	+ 8	+ 1	+ 9

Number Correct

——
20

Addition Test 4—Sums to 11, 12, 13, 14, and 15

5	4	10	8	10	6	5
+ 8	+ 9	+ 5	+ 7	+ 2	+ 8	+ 6

9	6	7	11	5	12	3
+ 2	+ 6	+ 4	+ 3	+ 9	+ 2	+ 8

4	13	6	13	3	9
+ 7	+ 2	+ 5	+ 1	+ 9	+ 6

Number Correct

——
20

Addition Test 5—Sums to 11, 12, 13, 14, and 15

8 + 4	6 + 5	12 + 3	4 + 9	5 + 7	10 + 5	7 + 7
7 + 8	7 + 4	9 + 6	6 + 6	10 + 3	12 + 2	14 + 1
6 + 8	8 + 5	7 + 6	6 + 9	5 + 8	4 + 7	Number Correct — 20

Addition Test 6—Sums to 11, 12, 13, 14, and 15

3 + 9	6 + 6	7 + 7	8 + 7	10 + 3	13 + 1	6 + 5
1 + 14	7 + 5	8 + 3	5 + 6	9 + 4	6 + 8	10 + 5
4 + 8	3 + 10	4 + 7	7 + 6	12 + 3	9 + 5	Number Correct — 20

Addition Test 7—Sums to 11, 12, 13, 14, and 15

4 + 9	6 + 6	8 + 3	12 + 2	15 + 0	6 + 8	11 + 1
12 + 0	6 + 9	9 + 2	14 + 1	7 + 6	10 + 3	7 + 7
7 + 4	8 + 5	5 + 9	11 + 4	5 + 7	10 + 4	

Number Correct

‾‾‾‾
20

Addition Test 8—Sums to 11, 12, 13, 14, and 15

12 + 2	7 + 4	9 + 6	6 + 6	10 + 3	6 + 5	8 + 7
9 + 4	3 + 8	6 + 7	13 + 2	10 + 2	8 + 6	11 + 2
5 + 7	7 + 7	4 + 8	13 + 1	15 + 0	9 + 5	

Number Correct

‾‾‾‾
20

Addition Test 9—Sums to 11, 12, 13, 14, and 15

12	11	9	13	8	10	7
+ 3	+ 0	+ 4	+ 1	+ 5	+ 2	+ 6

11	9	4	6	3	5	1
+ 2	+ 2	+ 10	+ 9	+ 8	+ 7	+ 14

7	8	5	3	2	4	
+ 8	+ 6	+ 7	+ 10	+ 12	+ 8	

Number Correct

_____
20

Addition Test 10—Sums to 11, 12, 13, 14, and 15

13	5	3	1	4	6	8
+ 1	+ 6	+ 9	+ 12	+ 8	+ 5	+ 7

6	7	10	11	4	6	6
+ 6	+ 7	+ 5	+ 3	+ 7	+ 8	+ 9

11	9	5	7	5	9	
+ 0	+ 6	+ 8	+ 6	+ 7	+ 2	

Number Correct

_____
20

Addition Test 1—Sums to 16, 17, 18, 19, and 20

16	7	9	13	15	18	9
+ 3	+ 9	+ 10	+ 4	+ 2	+ 2	+ 7

19	8	20	17	10	10	17
+ 1	+ 9	+ 0	+ 0	+ 10	+ 8	+ 1

16	8	15	14	10	9
+ 2	+ 8	+ 3	+ 2	+ 7	+ 9

Number Correct

___
20

Addition Test 2—Sums to 16, 17, 18, 19, and 20

13	19	7	15	15	16	3
+ 4	+ 1	+ 9	+ 1	+ 4	+ 1	+ 17

19	10	16	13	5	8	10
+ 1	+ 8	+ 3	+ 3	+ 12	+ 8	+ 7

20	15	9	7	10	9
+ 0	+ 2	+ 9	+ 10	+ 10	+ 8

Number Correct

___
20

Addition Test 3—Sums to 16, 17, 18, 19, and 20

12	15	16	4	7	8	10
+ 4	+ 1	+ 3	+ 13	+ 9	+ 10	+ 7

20	18	19	15	8	9	10
+ 0	+ 1	+ 1	+ 2	+ 8	+ 8	+ 10

18	9	16	9	12	17	Number Correct
+ 2	+ 9	+ 1	+ 7	+ 5	+ 2	

_____
20

Addition Test 4—Sums to 16, 17, 18, 19, and 20

15	9	5	17	8	17	8
+ 1	+ 7	+ 12	+ 2	+ 9	+ 1	+ 8

16	18	10	15	17	9	14
+ 3	+ 2	+ 7	+ 2	+ 3	+ 9	+ 2

19	8	13	20	7	18	Number Correct
+ 1	+ 10	+ 3	+ 0	+ 10	+ 1	

_____
20

Addition Test 5—Sums to 16, 17, 18, 19, and 20

17 + 3	12 + 5	9 + 10	7 + 10	10 + 7	8 + 8	12 + 4
10 + 10	8 + 9	16 + 2	17 + 0	1 + 16	10 + 8	13 + 7
7 + 9	4 + 12	15 + 3	8 + 10	10 + 9	9 + 9	

Number Correct

___
20

Addition Test 6—Sums to 16, 17, 18, 19, and 20

9 + 8	14 + 6	5 + 11	7 + 12	15 + 4	16 + 1	3 + 17
19 + 1	10 + 8	16 + 3	13 + 4	8 + 8	10 + 7	8 + 11
9 + 9	11 + 6	14 + 5	2 + 15	7 + 13	15 + 2	

Number Correct

___
20

Addition Test 7—Sums to 16, 17, 18, 19, and 20

13 + 4	10 + 7	12 + 5	16 + 2	2 + 14	9 + 10	12 + 4
9 + 11	8 + 9	13 + 7	17 + 2	10 + 10	9 + 8	11 + 7
16 + 2	11 + 8	15 + 3	8 + 8	5 + 12	9 + 9	Number Correct 20

Addition Test 8—Sums to 16, 17, 18, 19, and 20

13 + 3	18 + 2	16 + 1	10 + 10	14 + 4	10 + 9	9 + 9
17 + 1	10 + 8	14 + 3	8 + 8	19 + 0	7 + 9	10 + 7
19 + 1	17 + 0	6 + 10	9 + 8	17 + 2	16 + 2	Number Correct 20

Addition Test 9—Sums to 16, 17, 18, 19, and 20

16 + 3	14 + 5	9 + 10	9 + 9	15 + 2	3 + 17	12 + 4
10 + 10	8 + 9	18 + 1	17 + 0	1 + 16	10 + 8	11 + 7
16 + 2	7 + 9	15 + 3	8 + 8	9 + 8	19 + 1	Number Correct ___ 20

Addition Test 10—Sums to 16, 17, 18, 19, and 20

13 + 4	14 + 6	5 + 12	8 + 8	15 + 4	16 + 1	3 + 17
19 + 1	10 + 8	16 + 3	13 + 4	9 + 8	8 + 11	10 + 7
10 + 10	15 + 2	9 + 9	2 + 15	7 + 13	16 + 2	Number Correct ___ 20

How Am I Doing?

Addition Tests—Sums to 1, 2, 3, 4, and 5

Number correct	Test 1	Test 2	Test 3	Test 4	Test 5	Test 6	Test 7	Test 8	Test 9	Test 10
20										
19										
18										
17										
16										
15										
14										
13										
12										
11										
10										
9										
8										
7										
6										
5										
4										
3										
2										
1										

Addition Tests—Sums to 6, 7, 8, 9, and 10

Number correct	Test 1	Test 2	Test 3	Test 4	Test 5	Test 6	Test 7	Test 8	Test 9	Test 10
20										
19										
18										
17										
16										
15										
14										
13										
12										
11										
10										
9										
8										
7										
6										
5										
4										
3										
2										
1										

How Am I Doing?

Addition Tests—Sums to 11, 12, 13, 14, and 15

Number correct	Test 1	Test 2	Test 3	Test 4	Test 5	Test 6	Test 7	Test 8	Test 9	Test 10
20										
19										
18										
17										
16										
15										
14										
13										
12										
11										
10										
9										
8										
7										
6										
5										
4										
3										
2										
1										

Addition Tests—Sums to 16, 17, 18, 19, and 20

Number correct	Test 1	Test 2	Test 3	Test 4	Test 5	Test 6	Test 7	Test 8	Test 9	Test 10
20										
19										
18										
17										
16										
15										
14										
13										
12										
11										
10										
9										
8										
7										
6										
5										
4										
3										
2										
1										

How to Use the Subtraction Table

The numbers in the dark border down the side show the rows. The numbers in the dark border at the top show the columns. You can use this table to subtract to find the difference of two numbers. For example, find the difference of 9 − 5.

Go down to the 9 row. Put your finger on the 9. Then slide your finger along the 9 row to the 5 column. The number in the square is your answer! So, 9 − 5 = 4.

If you find a blank space, that means you cannot subtract those two numbers.

−	0	1	2	3	4	5	6	7	8	9	10
0	0										
1	1	0									
2	2	1	0								
3	3	2	1	0							
4	4	3	2	1	0						
5	5	4	3	2	1	0					
6	6	5	4	3	2	1	0				
7	7	6	5	4	3	2	1	0			
8	8	7	6	5	4	3	2	1	0		
9	9	8	7	6	5	4	3	2	1	0	
10	10	9	8	7	6	5	4	3	2	1	0

Subtraction Test 1—Differences from 5, 4, 3, 2, and 1

5	4	2	5	4	3	1
− 2	− 3	− 1	− 4	− 0	− 3	− 1

3	5	2	4	5	4	5
− 0	− 5	− 2	− 2	− 1	− 4	− 3

4	2	3	1	3	5
− 1	− 0	− 2	− 0	− 1	− 0

Number Correct

———
20

Subtraction Test 2—Differences from 5, 4, 3, 2, and 1

2	5	3	4	5	4	3
− 1	− 4	− 2	− 0	− 3	− 2	− 0

5	4	5	1	3	2	4
− 1	− 1	− 5	− 1	− 3	− 0	− 3

3	5	4	5	2	1
− 1	− 2	− 4	− 0	− 2	− 0

Number Correct

———
20

Subtraction Test 3—Differences from 5, 4, 3, 2, and 1

2	5	3	5	1	4	3
− 2	− 3	− 1	− 5	− 0	− 3	− 2

5	1	4	2	3	2	5
− 2	− 1	− 2	− 1	− 3	− 0	− 1

3	4	5	4	5	4	
− 0	− 4	− 0	− 1	− 4	− 0	

Number Correct

———
20

Subtraction Test 4—Differences from 5, 4, 3, 2, and 1

4	5	3	1	3	2	3
− 4	− 3	− 2	− 0	− 3	− 2	− 1

5	2	5	4	3	1	2
− 2	− 1	− 5	− 1	− 0	− 1	− 0

4	5	4	5	4	5	
− 3	− 0	− 0	− 1	− 2	− 4	

Number Correct

———
20

Subtraction Test 5—Differences from 5, 4, 3, 2, and 1

5	3	4	1	2	3	5
− 2	− 0	− 1	− 0	− 1	− 2	− 5

4	3	2	4	3	2	5
− 0	− 1	− 0	− 2	− 3	− 2	− 3

5	1	4	5	4	5
− 1	− 1	− 4	− 0	− 3	− 4

Number Correct

___
20

Subtraction Test 6—Differences from 5, 4, 3, 2, and 1

4	5	2	5	4	1	3
− 0	− 4	− 2	− 1	− 1	− 0	− 1

2	3	5	3	1	4	3
− 0	− 2	− 5	− 0	− 1	− 2	− 3

5	4	5	4	5	2
− 3	− 4	− 2	− 3	− 0	− 1

Number Correct

___
20

Subtraction Test 7—Differences from 5, 4, 3, 2, and 1

4	3	5	3	2	4	1
− 1	− 3	− 4	− 2	− 0	− 3	− 0

5	2	1	5	5	4	3
− 0	− 2	− 1	− 3	− 5	− 4	− 0

3	4	5	4	2	5
− 1	− 2	− 2	− 0	− 1	− 1

Number Correct

_____
20

Subtraction Test 8—Differences from 5, 4, 3, 2, and 1

4	5	3	1	5	2	3
− 4	− 3	− 2	− 0	− 4	− 2	− 1

5	2	5	4	3	5	4
− 2	− 1	− 0	− 1	− 0	− 5	− 2

5	4	1	2	3	4
− 1	− 3	− 1	− 0	− 3	− 0

Number Correct

_____
20

Subtraction Test 9—Differences from 5, 4, 3, 2, and 1

3	4	5	2	1	5	4
− 3	− 0	− 5	− 1	− 0	− 2	− 1

4	3	2	5	3	1	3
− 4	− 2	− 0	− 3	− 0	− 1	− 1

5	4	5	2	5	4
− 1	− 3	− 0	− 2	− 4	− 2

Number Correct

___
20

Subtraction Test 10—Differences from 5, 4, 3, 2, and 1

5	4	3	2	1	3	5
− 4	− 1	− 3	− 1	− 0	− 2	− 3

2	3	5	4	2	4	5
− 2	− 0	− 2	− 0	− 0	− 2	− 5

5	4	3	1	4	5
− 0	− 3	− 1	− 1	− 4	− 1

Number Correct

___
20

Subtraction Test 1—Differences from 10, 9, 8, 7, and 6

10	8	6	7	10	9	6
− 9	− 6	− 3	− 4	− 2	− 6	− 2

7	10	9	8	6	7	10
− 7	− 5	− 8	− 3	− 5	− 3	− 1

8	6	10	9	7	8
− 7	− 0	− 8	− 5	− 1	− 2

Number Correct

_____
20

Subtraction Test 2—Differences from 10, 9, 8, 7, and 6

10	8	9	7	10	6	8
− 6	− 4	− 2	− 0	− 3	− 4	− 1

6	7	8	10	7	9	10
− 6	− 2	− 5	− 4	− 5	− 1	− 7

8	9	7	8	9	10
− 8	− 3	− 6	− 0	− 7	−10

Number Correct

_____
20

Subtraction Test 3—Differences from 10, 9, 8, 7, and 6

9	10	8	9	6	9	7
− 4	− 0	− 3	− 0	− 4	− 9	− 7

8	10	7	6	9	8	10
− 6	− 8	− 2	− 3	− 7	− 2	− 1

10	6	10	9	8	7
− 7	− 1	−10	− 6	− 1	− 5

Number Correct

___
20

Subtraction Test 4—Differences from 10, 9, 8, 7, and 6

10	6	7	10	8	9	7
− 4	− 0	− 3	− 9	− 4	− 2	− 4

6	8	10	9	7	9	7
− 2	− 5	− 3	− 5	− 6	− 1	− 0

9	10	7	6	8	6
− 3	− 2	− 1	− 5	− 7	− 6

Number Correct

___
20

Subtraction Test 5—Differences from 10, 9, 8, 7, and 6

10	8	9	10	8	9	10
− 5	− 8	− 0	− 6	− 0	− 4	− 0

9	7	9	6	10	7	8
− 8	− 3	− 9	− 0	− 3	− 5	− 1

7	9	6	10	8	7
− 6	− 7	− 2	− 8	− 3	− 2

Number Correct

_____
20

Subtraction Test 6—Differences from 10, 9, 8, 7, and 6

9	10	8	6	7	10	9
− 1	− 4	− 5	− 6	− 0	− 7	− 5

8	6	10	7	9	8	7
− 2	− 3	− 1	− 4	− 6	− 4	− 7

6	9	6	8	10	9
− 4	− 8	− 1	− 7	− 5	− 0

Number Correct

_____
20

Subtraction Test 7—Differences from 10, 9, 8, 7, and 6

8	10	8	9	10	9	7
− 0	− 9	− 6	− 2	− 6	− 4	− 1

6	9	8	6	9	10	8
− 5	− 3	− 8	− 2	− 9	− 2	− 1

7	9	6	10	8	7
− 7	− 0	− 6	− 10	− 3	− 4

Number Correct

___
20

Subtraction Test 8—Differences from 10, 9, 8, 7, and 6

6	8	7	10	7	9	6
− 3	− 4	− 5	− 6	− 0	− 2	− 1

7	6	10	8	9	6	7
− 2	− 5	− 1	− 5	− 4	− 0	− 6

8	9	7	9	10	9
− 7	− 5	− 3	− 6	− 8	− 1

Number Correct

___
20

Subtraction Test 9—Differences from 10, 9, 8, 7, and 6

10	7	9	8	6	10	8
− 7	− 1	− 3	− 2	− 4	− 5	− 8

9	8	6	7	10	9	8
− 7	− 0	− 2	− 7	− 4	− 8	− 1

10	9	7	10	8	10
− 3	− 9	− 3	− 2	− 3	− 0

Number Correct

———
20

Subtraction Test 10—Differences from 10, 9, 8, 7, and 6

10	8	9	8	6	10	8
− 10	− 2	− 6	− 7	− 4	− 1	− 1

6	9	10	7	8	9	10
− 0	− 1	− 8	− 2	− 5	− 0	− 4

10	8	6	9	10	6
− 5	− 6	− 1	− 5	− 7	− 5

Number Correct

———
20

Subtraction Test 1—Differences from 15, 14, 13, 12, and 11

11	14	12	15	12	13	15
− 0	− 6	− 8	− 7	− 5	− 2	− 9

13	11	15	13	14	15	11
− 8	− 10	− 6	− 9	− 1	− 5	− 2

15	12	14	11	13	11
− 2	− 0	− 7	− 3	− 7	− 8

Number Correct

_____
20

Subtraction Test 2—Differences from 15, 14, 13, 12, and 11

15	14	13	12	11	15	13
− 1	− 4	− 2	− 6	− 5	− 2	− 1

14	11	12	13	15	11	12
− 2	− 3	− 1	− 5	− 9	− 1	− 4

13	12	11	15	14	13
− 10	− 8	− 4	− 6	− 5	− 7

Number Correct

_____
20

Subtraction Test 3—Differences from 15, 14, 13, 12, and 11

13	15	12	14	11	14	15
− 0	− 7	− 6	− 4	− 9	− 7	− 5

14	11	15	13	14	15	11
− 6	− 3	− 2	− 3	− 2	− 1	− 2

15	12	14	11	13	11	Number Correct
− 8	− 8	− 9	− 7	− 2	− 4	

20

Subtraction Test 4—Differences from 15, 14, 13, 12, and 11

11	12	13	14	15	11	13
− 9	− 4	− 2	− 6	− 5	− 2	− 1

12	11	12	13	15	11	12
−10	− 3	− 1	− 6	− 8	− 5	− 7

13	12	11	15	14	13	Number Correct
− 7	− 8	−10	− 6	− 5	− 4	

20

Subtraction Test 5—Differences from 15, 14, 13, 12, and 11

15	13	11	12	14	12	14
− 7	− 5	− 5	− 1	− 5	− 6	− 6

11	13	14	15	13	14	11
− 9	− 10	− 7	− 1	− 2	− 3	− 3

12	15	14	11	13	11	Number Correct
− 3	− 10	− 4	− 7	− 6	− 1	

____
20

Subtraction Test 6—Differences from 15, 14, 13, 12, and 11

14	12	11	13	15	12	13
− 1	− 4	− 6	− 7	− 6	− 2	− 9

15	13	14	12	13	11	15
− 2	− 3	− 8	− 9	− 2	− 4	− 7

13	11	12	15	14	13	Number Correct
− 1	− 2	− 3	− 5	− 4	− 10	

____
20

Subtraction Test 7—Differences from 15, 14, 13, 12, and 11

12	14	12	15	12	13	15
− 4	− 10	− 12	− 9	− 5	− 3	− 7

15	12	15	13	14	11	12
− 2	− 10	− 8	− 2	− 6	− 4	− 1

14	15	13	11	13	15
− 5	− 10	− 6	− 7	− 5	− 5

Number Correct

———
20

Subtraction Test 8—Differences from 15, 14, 13, 12, and 11

13	14	15	12	11	15	13
− 1	− 4	− 2	− 6	− 7	− 12	− 7

14	11	12	13	15	11	12
− 2	− 3	− 1	− 9	− 9	− 1	− 4

12	15	13	15	14	13
− 9	− 8	− 4	− 6	− 5	− 0

Number Correct

———
20

Subtraction Test 9—Differences from 15, 14, 13, 12, and 11

15	13	12	15	14	11	15
− 6	− 5	− 8	− 1	− 7	− 10	− 9

12	11	15	14	13	15	14
− 9	− 7	− 2	− 9	− 7	− 5	− 1

11	13	14	15	13	12
− 3	− 9	− 2	− 7	− 1	− 2

Number Correct

$\overline{20}$

Subtraction Test 10—Differences from 15, 14, 13, 12, and 11

15	14	13	12	11	13	15
− 6	− 4	− 2	− 6	− 2	− 10	− 1

14	13	12	11	15	11	12
− 2	− 3	− 1	− 10	− 7	− 1	− 4

13	12	11	15	14	13
− 6	− 8	− 4	− 2	− 5	− 7

Number Correct

$\overline{20}$

Subtraction Test 1—Differences from 20, 19, 18, 17, and 16

19	18	20	17	16	18	17
− 9	− 2	− 1	− 1	− 7	− 5	− 7

16	18	17	20	16	18	19
− 0	− 8	− 9	− 2	− 9	− 10	− 1

17	20	18	16	18	19
− 2	− 10	− 9	− 8	− 1	− 2

Number Correct

___
20

Subtraction Test 2—Differences from 20, 19, 18, 17, and 16

20	16	19	17	18	16	17
− 1	− 10	− 2	− 1	− 1	− 2	− 9

18	19	16	18	19	20	17
− 2	− 1	− 8	− 10	− 9	− 10	− 7

16	17	20	16	17	18
− 1	− 2	− 2	− 6	− 5	− 9

Number Correct

___
20

Subtraction Test 3—Differences from 20, 19, 18, 17, and 16

16	20	19	17	18	16	17
− 6	− 1	− 9	− 1	− 9	− 2	− 7

18	19	17	20	16	18	17
− 10	− 10	− 10	− 2	− 8	− 2	− 9

19	16	20	18	19	17
− 2	− 7	− 10	− 8	− 11	− 2

Number Correct

———
20

Subtraction Test 4—Differences from 20, 19, 18, 17, and 16

16	18	19	20	16	18	17
− 1	− 9	− 2	− 2	− 6	− 2	− 9

17	16	19	18	19	17	20
− 2	− 10	− 1	− 8	− 9	− 1	− 1

18	20	16	19	17	16
− 1	− 10	− 8	− 10	− 7	− 0

Number Correct

———
20

Subtraction Test 5—Differences from 20, 19, 18, 17, and 16

19	17	18	16	20	19	16
− 9	− 2	− 8	− 9	− 10	− 2	− 8

20	18	16	19	17	16	18
− 1	− 1	− 7	− 10	− 8	− 12	− 10

19	16	17	18	16	17	Number Correct
− 1	− 6	− 7	− 9	− 1	− 11	

20

Subtraction Test 6—Differences from 20, 19, 18, 17, and 16

19	16	18	17	18	20	16
− 1	− 8	− 2	− 9	− 10	− 2	− 1

16	17	20	18	19	16	17
− 2	− 12	− 17	− 9	− 9	− 9	− 2

16	18	17	16	20	17	Number Correct
− 10	− 8	− 7	− 7	− 10	− 1	

20

Subtraction Test 7—Differences from 20, 19, 18, 17, and 16

20	19	17	16	18	19	17
− 10	− 2	− 8	− 9	− 1	− 10	− 9

18	16	19	17	20	18	16
− 8	− 10	− 9	− 2	− 14	− 10	− 1

19	18	17	18	16	20
− 12	− 15	− 7	− 9	− 14	− 15

Number Correct

___

20

Subtraction Test 8—Differences from 20, 19, 18, 17, and 16

16	17	18	20	18	17	16
− 1	− 9	− 2	− 13	− 9	− 2	− 8

17	16	19	16	19	20	18
− 12	− 10	− 9	− 7	− 2	− 19	− 10

18	20	16	18	17	16
− 1	− 10	− 9	− 8	− 7	− 16

Number Correct

___

20

Subtraction Test 9—Differences from 20, 19, 18, 17, and 16

18	19	16	17	16	19	16
− 9	− 2	− 8	− 7	− 7	− 10	− 6

20	16	19	18	17	20	18
− 10	− 10	− 9	− 8	− 9	− 2	− 1

17	20	18	16	19	18
− 8	− 1	− 10	− 12	− 1	− 7

Number Correct

_____
20

Subtraction Test 10—Differences from 20, 19, 18, 17, and 16

18	17	19	20	19	16	17
− 1	− 8	− 2	− 8	− 9	− 7	− 1

19	16	17	18	16	20	18
− 10	− 9	− 10	− 8	− 6	− 15	− 10

17	16	18	19	20	17
− 7	− 8	− 9	− 5	− 13	− 9

Number Correct

_____
20

How Am I Doing?

Subtraction Tests—Differences from 5, 4, 3, 2, and 1

Number correct	Test 1	Test 2	Test 3	Test 4	Test 5	Test 6	Test 7	Test 8	Test 9	Test 10
20										
19										
18										
17										
16										
15										
14										
13										
12										
11										
10										
9										
8										
7										
6										
5										
4										
3										
2										
1										

Subtraction Tests—Differences from 10, 9, 8, 7, and 6

Number correct	Test 1	Test 2	Test 3	Test 4	Test 5	Test 6	Test 7	Test 8	Test 9	Test 10
20										
19										
18										
17										
16										
15										
14										
13										
12										
11										
10										
9										
8										
7										
6										
5										
4										
3										
2										
1										

How Am I Doing?

Subtraction Tests—Differences from 15, 14, 13, 12, and 11

Number correct	Test 1	Test 2	Test 3	Test 4	Test 5	Test 6	Test 7	Test 8	Test 9	Test 10
20										
19										
18										
17										
16										
15										
14										
13										
12										
11										
10										
9										
8										
7										
6										
5										
4										
3										
2										
1										

Subtraction Tests—Differences from 20, 19, 18, 17, and 16

Number correct	Test 1	Test 2	Test 3	Test 4	Test 5	Test 6	Test 7	Test 8	Test 9	Test 10
20										
19										
18										
17										
16										
15										
14										
13										
12										
11										
10										
9										
8										
7										
6										
5										
4										
3										
2										
1										

 **Aa**

Trace and print. Circle your best A or a on each line.

A A A A A A A A

A

A

a a a a a a a a

a

a

© Chalkboard Publishing

Bb

Trace and print. Circle your best B or b on each line.

Cc

Trace and print. Circle your best C or c on each line.

Dd

Trace and print. Circle your best D or d on each line.

Ee

Trace and print. Circle your best E or e on each line.

Ff

Trace and print. Circle your best F or f on each line.

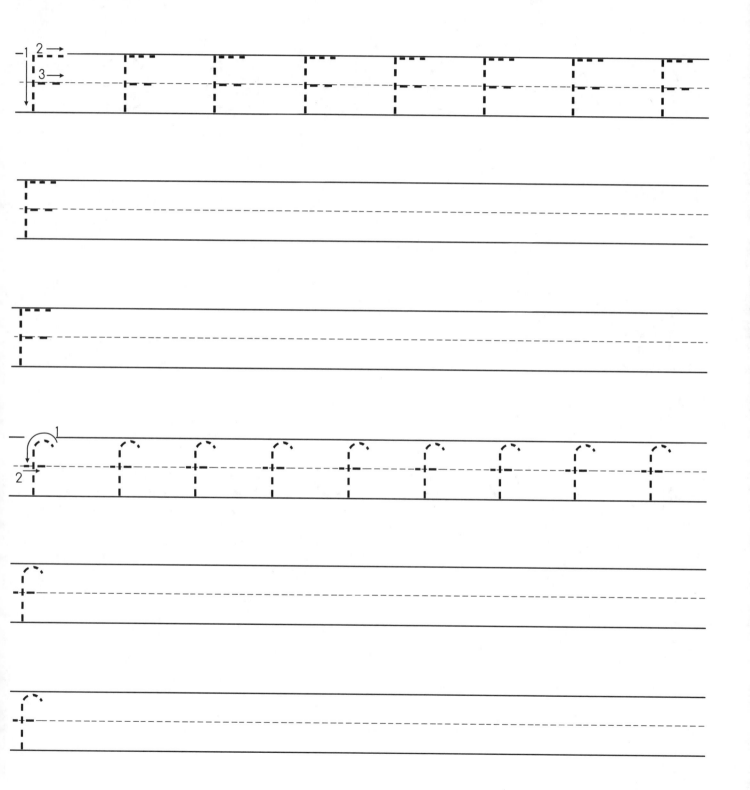

Gg

Trace and print. Circle your best G or g on each line.

Hh Trace and print. Circle your best H or h on each line.

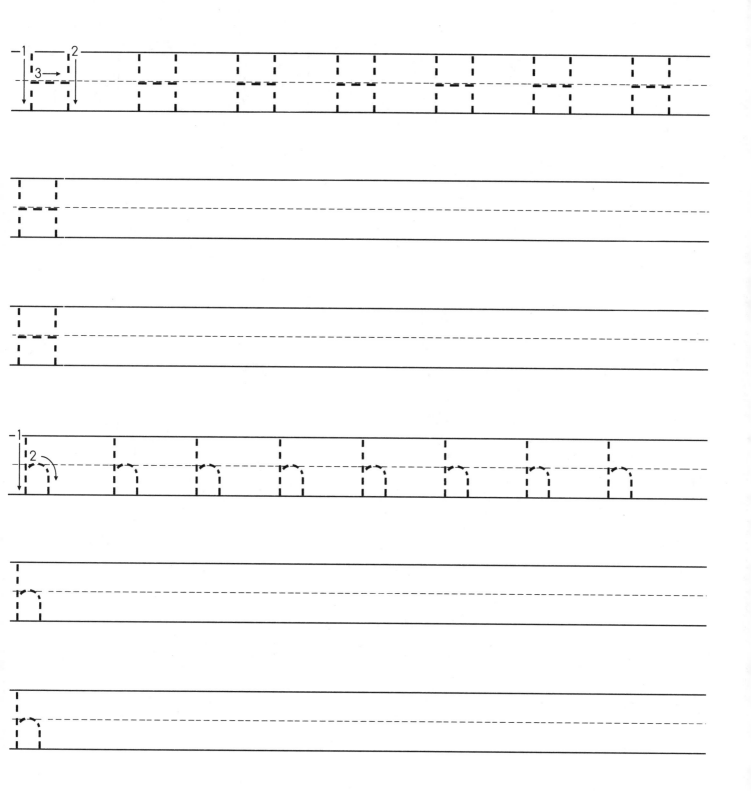

I i

Trace and print. Circle your best I or i on each line.

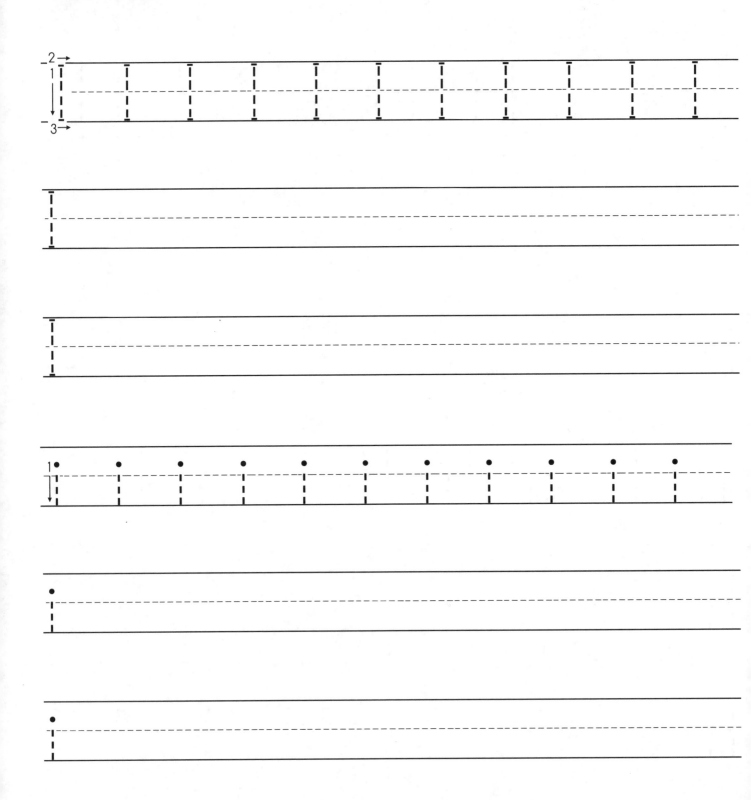

Jj

Trace and print. Circle your best J or j on each line.

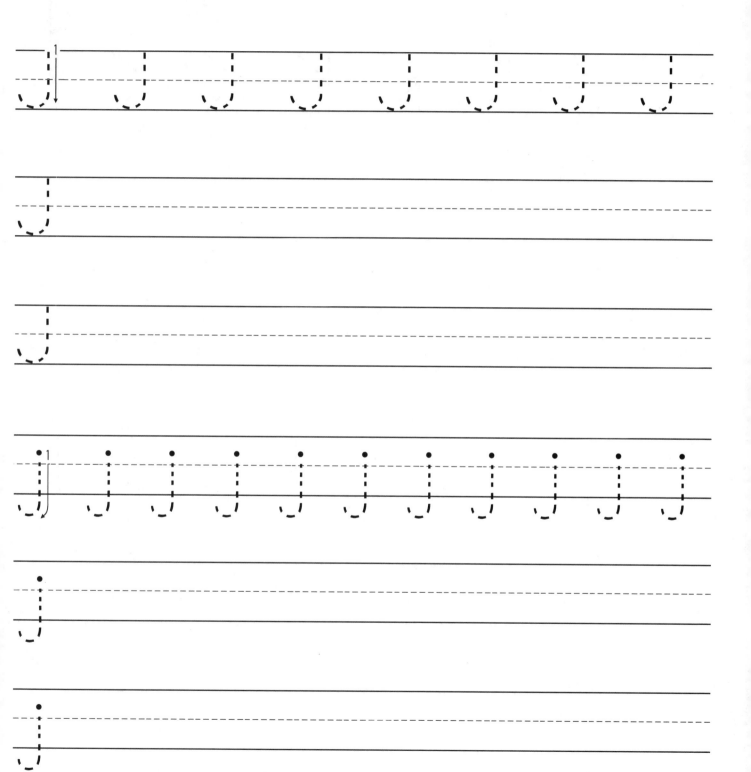

Kk

Trace and print. Circle your best K or k on each line.

Trace and print. Circle your best L or l on each line.

Mm Trace and print. Circle your best M or m on each line.

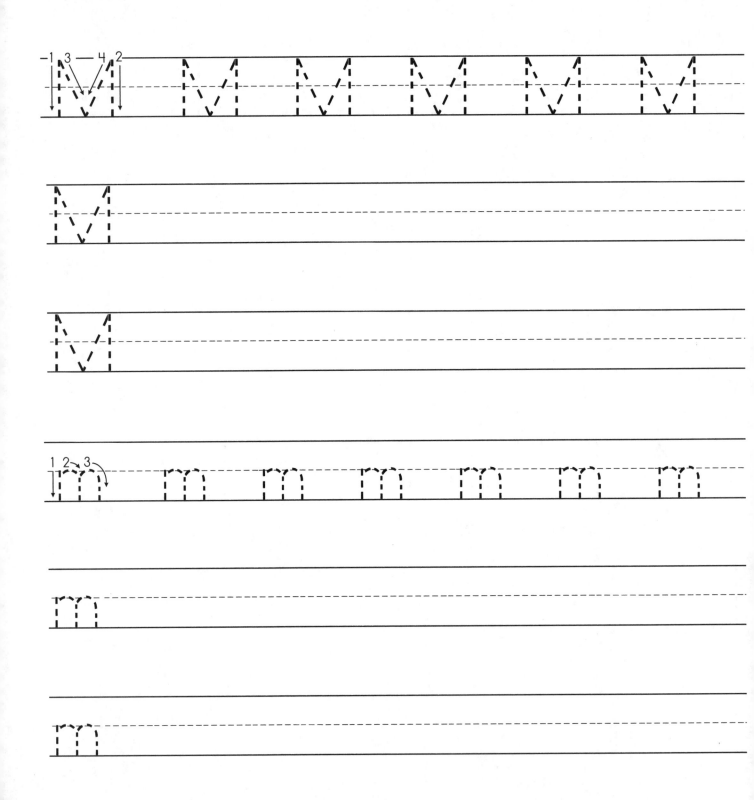

© Chalkboard Publishing

Nn

Trace and print. Circle your best N or n on each line.

 Trace and print. Circle your best ◯ or o on each line.

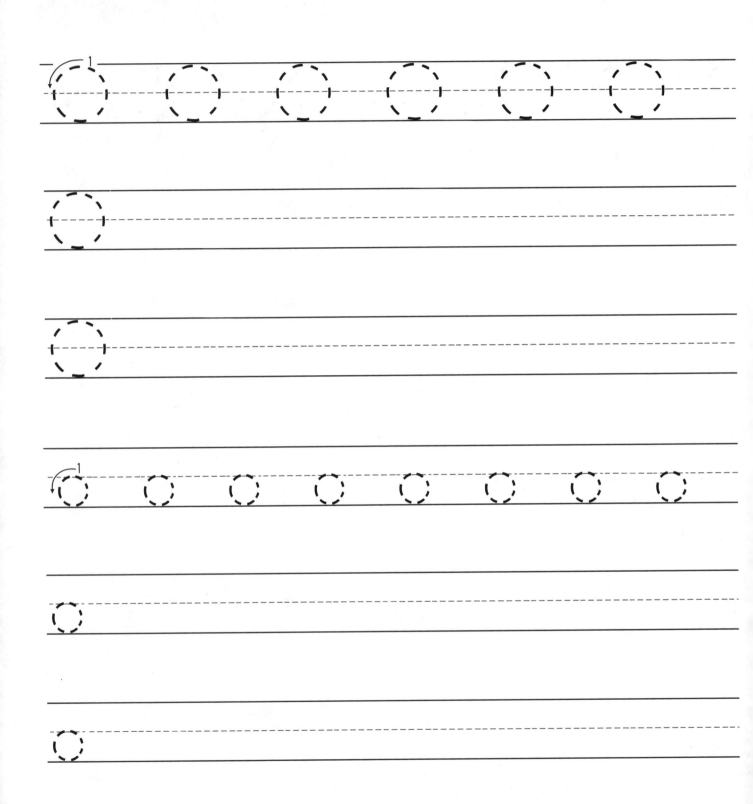

Trace and print. Circle your best P or p on each line.

P P P P P P P P

P

P

P P P P P P P P

p

p

Trace and print. Circle your best Q or q on each line.

Rr

Trace and print. Circle your best R or r on each line.

Ss

Trace and print. Circle your best S or s on each line.

Trace and print. Circle your best T or t on each line.

Uu

Trace and print. Circle your best U or u on each line.

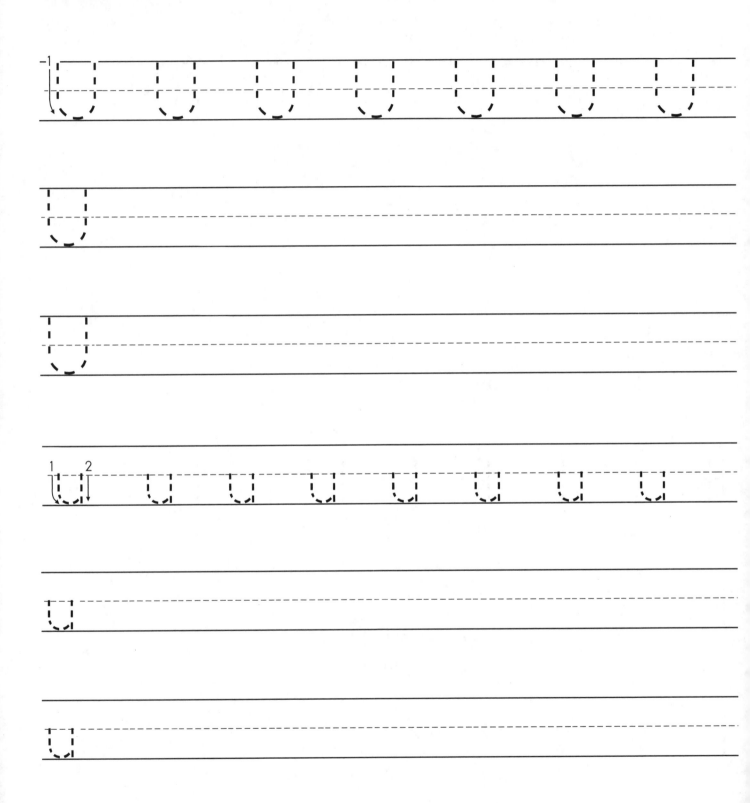

Trace and print. Circle your best V or v on each line.

Trace and print. Circle your best W or w on each line.

Trace and print. Circle your best X or x on each line.

Trace and print. Circle your best Y or y on each line.

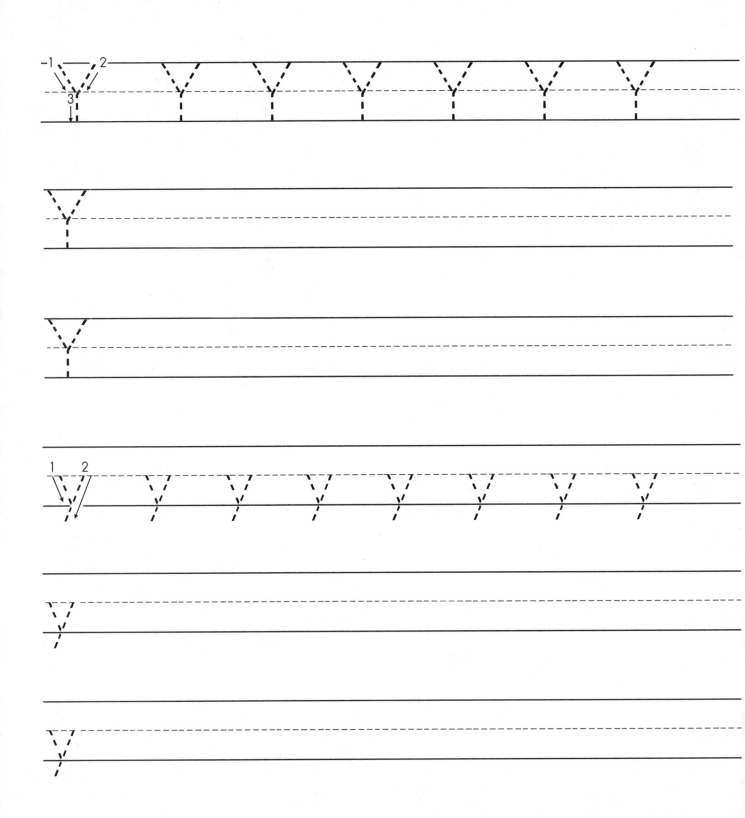

Zz

Trace and print. Circle your best Z or z on each line.

What Is a Sentence?

A **sentence** is a group of words that tells a complete idea.
Every **sentence** always begins with a **capital letter**.

Example: The dog runs fast.

1. Use a ✓ to mark the groups of words that make a sentence. Use an X to mark the groups of words that do not make a sentence .

   a) I like ice cream. _____

   b) is that _____

   c) the big dog

   d) He sat down on the mat. _____

   e) red hat _____

   f) She likes to play tag. _____

2. Write your own sentences.

   a) _____

   _____

   b) _____

   _____

Exploring Kinds of Sentences

A **telling** sentence ends with a **period**.

Example: Ken goes to the park.

An **asking** sentence ends with a **question mark**.

Example: Would you like to go to the park?

A sentence that shows strong feeling, such as excitement, joy, or anger, ends with an **exclamation mark**.

Examples: I love the park!   Ouch!   I can't wait!

A **command** sentence tells someone to do something.

It can end with a **period** or with an **exclamation mark**.

Examples: Take off your boots.   Watch out!

1. Write the correct punctuation at the end of each sentence.

a) Would you like a slice of pizza____

b) Put the basket on the table____

c) Hooray, we are going to the zoo____

d) Are you going to the library____

e) The girls are watching the parade____

f) Be careful____

g) What is your favourite season____

Exploring Kinds of Sentences (continued)

2. Write an example of each kind of sentence. Be sure to include the correct punctuation at the end of each sentence.

a) Telling sentence:

_____

_____

b) Asking sentence:

_____

_____

c) Sentence that shows strong feeling:

_____

_____

d) Command sentence:

_____

_____

Making a Noun Collage

A **noun** is a word that names a person, place, or thing.

Create a noun collage! Cut out pictures of nouns from magazines or flyers and glue them into the correct category.

People

Places

Things

Nouns: Am I a Person, Place, or Thing?

A **noun** is a word that names a person, place, or thing.

1. Colour the people red. Colour the places blue.
   Colour the things green.

home	girl	beach	yo-yo
fork	pencil	dog	teacher
backyard	toy	blanket	student
farm	cheese	grandma	park

© Chalkboard Publishing

Proper Nouns Need a Capital Letter

Nouns that always begin with a capital letter are called **proper nouns**.

The following kinds of nouns always begin with a capital letter:

- specific places, such as a **country, province, city,** or **town.** *Example: Canada*

- names of **holidays.** *Example: Canada Day*

- names of **people** or **pets.** *Example: Fluffy*

- names of the **days of the week** and the **months of the year.** *Examples: Monday and June*

1. Use proper nouns to complete the sentence.

   a) My dog's name is _____.

   b) I go to school on _____.

2. Write three proper nouns.

   _____

   _____

   _____

Plural Nouns

A **plural** noun names more than one person, place, or thing.

Add **s** to make most nouns **plural**.

Example: dog ⟶ dogs

---

1. Write the plural for each noun by adding **s**.

a) cat ⟶ _____ b) bird ⟶ _____

c) pig ⟶ _____ d) egg ⟶ _____

e) kid ⟶ _____ f) bell ⟶ _____

g) nest ⟶ _____ h) job ⟶ _____

Some nouns use a new word to name more than one.

Example: goose ⟶ geese

---

2. Write the correct word to name more than one.

a) person _____

b) man _____

c) tooth _____

Plural Nouns (continued)

A **plural** noun names more than one person, place, or thing.

Add **es** to nouns that end with **sh**, **ch**, **x**, or **s**.

Examples: fish ⟶ fishes

watch ⟶ watches

mix ⟶ mixes

glass ⟶ glasses

1. Write the plural for each noun by adding **es**.

a) witch ⟶ _____

b) wish ⟶ _____

c) glass ⟶ _____

d) rash ⟶ _____

e) bus ⟶ _____

f) lunch ⟶ _____

g) box ⟶ _____

h) dish ⟶ _____

Making a Verb Collage

Verbs are action words.

Examples: run, play, sit

Cut out pictures from magazines and flyers that represent verbs. Paste them into the box below.

Compound Words

Compound words are two words that are joined together to make a new word.

Example: *rain* + *bow* = *rainbow*

1. Complete the compound words.

   a) butter   +   fly   = _____

   b) cup   +   cake   = _____

   c) back   +   pack   = _____

   d) foot   +   ball   = _____

   e) sun   +   shine   = _____

   f) snow   +   ball   = _____

   g) bull   +   frog   = _____

2. Make your own compound word.

   _____ + _____ = _____

Reading Comprehension Tips

Reading comprehension is the cornerstone of a student's academic success. By completing the activities in this book, students will benefit from a wide variety of opportunities to practice engaging with text as active readers who can self-monitor their understanding of what they have read.

Focus on the following while working with students:

Identifying the Purpose of the Text
- Is the main purpose of the text to inform, entertain, or persuade readers?

Understanding the Text
- What is the main idea of the text?
- What are the supporting details?
- Which parts are facts and which parts are opinions?

Analyzing the Text
- How does the reader's background knowledge enhance the text clues to help the reader answer questions about the text or draw conclusions?
- What inferences can be made by combining information from the text with what the reader already knows?
- How does the information in the text help the reader make predictions?
- What is the cause-and-effect relationship between events?

Making Connections
How can the reader support or extend understanding of the text by making a variety of connections?
- Text-to-self connections: How does this text remind me of my own life?
- Text-to-text connections: Have I read something like this before? How is this text similar to something I have read before? How is this text different from something I have read before?
- Text-to-world connections: What does this text remind me of in the real world?

Using Text Features
- How do different text features help the reader?

Text Features

Text features help the reader to understand the text better. Here is a list of text features with a brief explanation on how they help the reader.

Contents	Here the reader will find the title of each section, what page each text starts on within sections, and where to find specific information.
Chapter Title	The chapter title gives the reader an idea of what the text will be about. The chapter title is often followed by subheadings within the text.
Title and Subheading	The title or topic is found at the top of the page. The subheading is right above a paragraph. There may be more than one subheading in a text.
Map	Maps help the reader understand where something is happening. It is a visual representation of a location.
Diagram and Illustration	Diagrams and illustrations give the reader additional visual information about the text.
Label	A label tells the reader the title of a map, diagram, or illustration. Labels also draw attention to specific elements within a visual.
Caption	Captions are words that are placed underneath the visuals. Captions give the reader more information about the map, diagram, or illustration.
Fact Box	A fact box tells the reader extra information about the topic.
Table	A table presents text information in columns and rows in a concise and often comparative way.
Bold and Italic text	**Bold** and *italic* text are used to emphasize a word or words, and signify that this is important vocabulary.

Making Connections with What I Have Read

After reading...	It reminds me of...	This helps me make a connection to...
		☐ something else I have read ☐ myself ☐ the world around me
		☐ something else I have read ☐ myself ☐ the world around me
		☐ something else I have read ☐ myself ☐ the world around me
		☐ something else I have read ☐ myself ☐ the world around me

Table of Contents

Chapter 1: Introduction
Chapter 2: Chickens
Chapter 3: Pigs
Chapter 4: Cows
Chapter 5: Horses
Chapter 6: The Barn

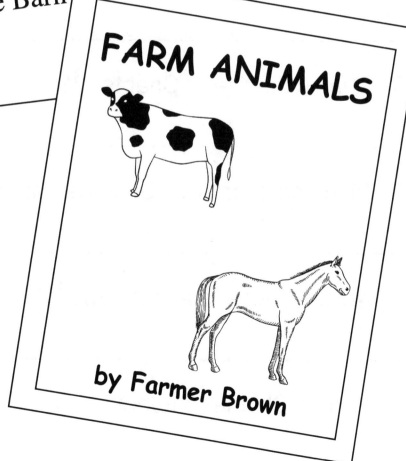

FARM ANIMALS

by Farmer Brown

"Using Text Features—Table of Contents"—Think About It!

1. What is the title of the book?

_____

2. Who is the author of the book?

_____

3. How many chapters are in the book?

_____

4. What is the title of Chapter 5?

_____

5. What is the title of Chapter 2?

_____

6. Which chapter tells about the barn?

_____

7. Which chapter is about cows?

_____

8. What is Chapter 3 about?

_____

Can We Get a Dog?

Dear Mom and Dad,

Can we get a dog?

Every dog needs a good home.

We can get one at the shelter.

I promise to take care of it.

I will feed it.

I will walk it.

I will play with it.

I will pick up after it.

A dog is a good pet for us to love.

Your son,

Andrew

"Can We Get a Dog?"—Think About It!

1. What is Andrew trying to get his parents to do?

_____

2. What did Andrew write to his parents? Circle the correct answer.

   A. a poster

   B. a letter

   C. a story

3. Where can Andrew's family get a dog?

_____

4. What are three arguments that Andrew uses?

_____

_____

_____

5. Do you think Andrew got a dog? Tell why.

_____

_____

Write a Letter

Write a letter to convince someone that it is a good idea to get a cat or dog.

(date) _____

Dear _____, (greeting)

(body)

_____

_____

_____

_____

_____

_____

_____

Checklist:

☐ I included a date.
☐ I included a greeting.
☐ I included a reason in my letter.
☐ I ended my letter with a closing and my name.

(closing) _____,

_____

(my name)

My New Boots

I am Kim. I love my new rain boots!

They are as red as a fire truck.

They are as shiny as a dime.

I like to wear them when I splash in puddles.

My new boots get wet but I stay dry.

Do you have boots? Draw a picture of you in your boots.

Write a sentence about when you need to wears boots.

_____

_____

"My New Boots"—Think About It!

1. Who has new boots?

_____

2. Write two details from the text to describe the rain boots.

_____

_____

3. When does Kim like to wear her red boots?

_____

4. What does Kim say happens when she splashes in puddles?

_____

_____

5. Name two other red things you know.

_____

_____

6. What other kind of boots can you have?

_____

_____

My Trip to a Farm

From: Kyle

To: Grandma

I went to a farm. I saw cows and pigs. I collected eggs.

I walked in the corn maze.

I picked some apples. I put them in a basket.

Maybe we can make a pie.

Love,

Kyle

"My Trip to a Farm"—Think About It!

1. Who wrote the email? How do you know?

_____

_____

2. Who will get the email?

_____

3. Who is telling the story? How do you know?

_____

_____

4. Where did Kyle go?

_____

5. Draw what Kyle asked his grandmother to make.

Little Brother, Big Brother

Rob has a little brother named Tim.

Rob is six. Tim is one.

Sometimes Tim is sad. Rob tries to make Tim smile.

Sometimes it works. Sometimes it does not work.

Rob's best friend Andy has a big brother named Dan.

Dan is twelve.

Sometimes Andy and Dan play games and have fun.

Sometimes Dan is mean to Andy. That is not fun!

Do you have a brother or sister? Draw a picture of the two of you below.

Write a sentence about your picture.

_____

"Little Brother, Big Brother"—Think About It!

1. How much older than Tim is Rob?

_____

2. How old is Dan?

_____

3. How do you think Rob tries to make Tim smile?

_____

_____

4. How do you think Dan is mean to Andy?

_____

_____

5. I would rather be a (big, small) _____
    brother or sister. Here are some reasons why.

_____

_____

_____

_____

A Hole in My Sock

This morning I saw a tiny hole in my sock.

My sock has the letter "L" on the sides. "L" stands for Lucy and that is my name.

At school, the hole got big. I put some tape over it.

At lunch time, the tape came off.

When I walked home, my big toe was showing.

Oh no! The hole is too big to fix now. Goodbye sock!

Draw a picture to go along with this text.

Write a sentence about your picture.

"A Hole in My Sock"—Think About It!

1. What does the letter "L" stand for on the girl's sock?

_____

2. What happened to the sock at school?

_____

3. How did Lucy try to fix her sock?

_____

4. What else could Lucy have done to fix her sock?

_____

_____

5. Can you think of two more girls' names that start with "L"?

_____

_____

6. Have you ever had a hole in your sock? What happened?

_____

_____

_____

Cookie Day

We will bake cookies today.

"What kind of cookies would you like to bake, Sara?" Mom asks me.

I like jam cookies. But Dad says jam is too sweet.

I like nut cookies. But nuts make Mom sick.

I also like sugar cookies.

Everyone in my family can eat sugar cookies!

That is what we will bake. Yum!

Draw a picture of your favourite cookie.

Write a sentence about your picture.

_____

"Cookie Day"—Think About It!

1. What are the three kinds of cookies Sara likes?

_____

_____

_____

2. Why can Sara not bake jam cookies?

_____

3. Why can Sara not bake cookies with nuts?

_____

4. Why kind of cookies does Sara bake? Circle the correct answer.

   A. jam
   B. sugar
   C. oatmeal

5. Write a sentence from the text that shows Sara is excited.

_____

_____

The Day My Cat Spoke

One morning, my cat Abby climbed up on my bed and said, "Get up, Ben."

"Did you just tell me to get up, Abby?" I asked.

"Yes. If you do not hurry, you will be late for school," said Abby.

I jumped out of bed. "Thanks, Abby."

"Meow," said Abby. "See you later."

My cat talked! It was wonderful!

"The Day My Cat Spoke" — Think About It!

1. What is the boy's name in the text?

_____

2. What is his cat's name?

_____

3. How do you think the boy felt when he heard his cat talk? Circle the correct answer.

   A. surprised

   B. upset

   C. bored

4. What did the cat tell the boy to do?

_____

5. Can you think of another word that means *wonderful*?

_____

6. What would you think if an animal spoke to you?

_____

_____

Ice Cream Fun

Do you like ice cream?

Make an ice cream sundae.

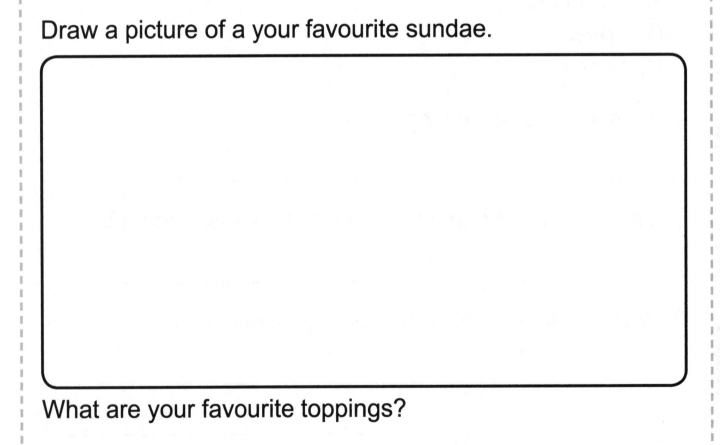

Here is what you do:

- First, put some ice cream into a bowl.
- Then, pour some syrup on it.
- Next, add some toppings.
- Finally, eat the ice cream!

Draw a picture of a your favourite sundae.

What are your favourite toppings?

_____

_____

"Ice Cream Fun"—Think About It!

1. What kind of ice cream do you like best? Tell why.

_____

_____

2. Name three things you need to make a sundae.

_____

_____

_____

3. Match the correct steps in making a sundae.

First,   add some
                                          toppings.

Then,   eat the ice cream!

Next,   pour some syrup
                                          on it.

Finally,   put some ice
                                          cream into a bowl.

Create a Poster

Create your own poster. What is the purpose of this poster?

☐ entertain   or   ☐ give information

Acrostic Poem

In an **acrostic** poem, the first letter of each line spells out a topic word or phrase. An acrostic poem describes the topic or even tells a short story about it.

Create your own acrostic poem.

Title _____

.... _____

.... _____

.... _____

.... _____

.... _____

.... _____

.... _____

.... _____

.... _____

Retell a Story

Read a story. Retell what happened in the story in your own words.

Story Title: _____

BEGINNING

_____

_____

_____

_____

_____

_____

Retell a Story (continued)

MIDDLE

_____

_____

_____

_____

_____

_____

Retell a Story (continued)

END

_____

_____

_____

_____

_____

_____

Story Planner

Write ideas for your story in this story planner.

Story Title: _____

Setting	Characters
Where will the story take place?	Who will be in the story?

Problem in the Story

What is the problem in the story?

Events in the Story

What happens in the story?

How the Problem Is Solved

How does the story end?

Adjectives for Writing

Category	Adjectives
Size	big, small, short, tall, fat, skinny, large, medium, slim, thin, slender, tiny, lean, scrawny, huge, gigantic, jumbo, plump, wee, wide, narrow
Shape	round, square, pointed, jagged, oval, chunky, curly, straight, curved, flat, twisted, heart-shaped, spiky, wavy, bent, tangled, messy
Colour	red, orange, yellow, green, blue, purple, pink, grey, white, black, brown, silver, gold
Age	young, old, new, baby, newborn
Sound	loud, quite, long, short, musical, surprising, soft, noisy, muffled, whispering, growling, grumbling
Light and Brightness	dull, bright, dark, light, clear, flashy, flashing, dim, faint, glowing, flickering, twinkly, twinkling, shiny, shining
Smell	good, bad, strong, sweet, salty, spicy, stinky, sour, delicious, yummy, fresh, rotten, rotting
Feel and Texture	soft, hard, smooth, rough, silky, fluffy, fuzzy, furry, wet, dry, bumpy, lumpy, scratchy, sweaty, slippery, slimy, gritty, dirty, sticky, gummy, jiggly, wiggly, squishy, watery, liquid, solid, rock hard, damp, stiff, firm
Taste	delicious, bitter, sweet, salty, tasty, spicy, yummy, bland, sour, strong
Speed and Movement	quick, quickly, fast, slow, slowly, rapid, rapidly, brisk, briskly, swift, swiftly, instant, instantly, late, lately
Temperature	hot, cold, icy, frosty, chilly, burning, boiling, steamy, sizzling, cool, warm, freezing, frozen, damp, humid, melting

Narrative Text: Write a Story

Story Title: _____

Beginning	☐ I wrote an attention-grabbing first sentence.
	☐ I introduced the main character.
	☐ I wrote about where the story takes place.

_____

_____

_____

_____

_____

_____

_____

_____

_____

_____

☐ I checked the spelling and punctuation.   ☐ I added adjectives.

Narrative Text: **Write a Story** (continued)

Middle ☐ I explained the problem in the story.

_____

_____

_____

_____

_____

_____

_____

_____

_____

_____

_____

_____

☐ I checked the spelling and punctuation. ☐ I added adjectives.

Narrative Text: Write a Story (continued)

Events	☐	I wrote about events that happen in the story before the problem is solved.

Event 1:

_____

_____

_____

_____

_____

Event 2:

_____

_____

_____

_____

_____

☐ **I checked the spelling and punctuation.** ☐ **I added adjectives.**

Narrative Text: Write a Story (continued)

Ending ☐ I explained how the problem was solved.

_____

_____

_____

_____

_____

_____

_____

_____

_____

_____

_____

_____

_____

☐ I checked the spelling and punctuation. ☐ I added adjectives.

Write a Letter

Write a letter to someone about an interesting day you had.

_____
(date)

_____ , (greeting)

(body)

_____

_____

_____

_____

_____

_____

_____

Checklist:

☐ I included a date.

☐ I included a greeting.

☐ I included a reason
in my letter.

(closing) _____ ,

☐ I ended my letter with a
closing and my name.

(signature) _____

Writing Prompts

1. Would you rather play at the playground or at the beach? Explain.

2. What are you proud of? Explain.

3. If I could be an animal for a day, I would be...

4. What would you wish for if you had three wishes? Explain.

5. Would you rather have a monkey for a pet, or a dog? Explain.

6. If you could be a superhero, what kind of special powers would you have? Explain.

7. Pretend you have a pet that talks. Write a story about what happens.

8. Would you rather travel by a train or an airplane? Explain.

9. If you could be a grownup at your school for a day, what would you do?

10. Invent and describe a new toy. What would it do? How would it work? Draw a labelled diagram of your new toy.

11. Create a grocery list. Be sure to include healthy foods.

12. Draw a picture of the weather. Write a weather report.

Procedural Text: How Do You Do That?

Write the steps on how to do something of your choice. For example, tell how to play a game, or give directions to get to a place.

This is how to _____

_____

First, _____

_____

Next, _____

_____

Then, _____

_____

After that, _____

_____

Finally, _____

_____

Picture Book Report

Title: _____

Author: _____

Illustrator: _____

Who is the main character in the story? This is who the story is mostly about.

_____

Draw a picture of the main character from the story.

Describe the main character.

_____

_____

What is the story about? What was the problem in the story?

_____

_____

Picture Book Report (continued)

Where does the story take place? This is called the setting in the story. Draw a picture that shows the setting.

Write about your picture.

_____

_____

How did the story end? How was the problem solved?

_____

_____

Do you think other people would enjoy this story? Explain your thinking.

_____

_____

My Favourite Part

Draw a picture of your favourite part of the story.

Write about why that was your favourite part of the story.

_____

_____

What do you think happened after the story ended?

_____

_____

What Is a Community?

A community is where people live, work, and spend time together.

A community can be your city, town, or village.

A community can be your street and neighbourhood.

Your school is a community.

Everyone lives in a community.

Many people belong to more than one community.

"What Is a Community?"—Think About It!

1. A community can be your _____, town, or village.

2. A community can be your _____and neighbourhood.

3. Your _____ is a community.

4. _____ lives in a community.

5. Many people belong to more than one

_____.

Thinking About My Community

A community is a place where people live, work, and spend time together.

1. What is the name of your community?

_____

2. Is your community big or small?

_____

3. Draw and label the different kinds of homes found in your community. Some different kinds of homes might include houses, apartments, townhouses, and houseboats.

4. Circle the ways people travel in your community.

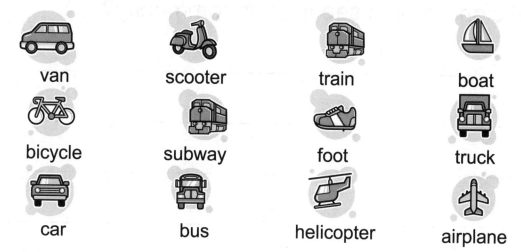

van   scooter   train   boat

bicycle   subway   foot   truck

car   bus   helicopter   airplane

5. What is your favourite way to travel? _____

6. Draw a public place people go to have fun in your community. Public places may include beach, park, library, sports arena, or playground.

7. Take a walk around your neighbourhood. What kinds of street signs do you see in your community?

_____

_____

_____

_____

_____

_____

8. What businesses are in your community?

_____

_____

_____

_____

_____

9. I think people choose to live in our community because...

_____

_____

_____

_____

_____

_____

10. What are some physical features in your community?
    Physical features may include mountains, lake, ocean,
    valley, or forest.

_____

_____

_____

_____

_____

11. This is a picture of _____

12. This person, place, or thing is important to the community because...

_____

_____

Word Search—Places Found in Some Communities

P	O	L	I	C	E	S	T	A	T	I	O	N	P	I
C	Q	H	O	M	E	S	T	I	W	P	C	P	H	W
I	Z	J	Z	L	E	J	U	Y	A	A	Y	L	O	Q
T	L	S	C	H	O	O	L	L	N	R	S	A	S	B
Y	M	Y	A	U	D	Z	R	J	L	K	B	Y	P	M
H	A	U	B	U	S	S	T	O	P	Y	U	G	I	U
A	L	R	A	I	R	P	O	R	T	B	Y	R	T	S
L	L	P	O	S	T	O	F	F	I	C	E	O	A	E
L	F	I	R	E	S	T	A	T	I	O	N	U	L	U
S	T	O	R	E	D	U	S	P	O	O	L	N	M	M
B	B	L	I	B	R	A	R	Y	W	K	K	D	X	Z

airport   homes   museum   pool
bus stop   hospital   park   post office
city hall   library   playground   school
fire station   mall   police staton   store

1. Think about your community. Name a place that is important to you. Give a reason.

_____

Needs and Wants

Needs are things that people must have to survive. An example of a need is clean water to drink.

Wants are things that people would like, but do not need to survive. An example of a want is a swimming pool.

1. Draw an example of a thing or a place that a community might need. Write a sentence about your picture.

_____

_____

2. Draw an example of a thing or place that a community might want. Write a sentence about your picture.

_____

_____

Our Community Collage

Look through magazines and brochures to find people, places, and things that are found in your community. Cut and paste these pictures into a collage in the space below.

My community is special because _____

_____

Keep Our Community Clean Poster

Create a poster encouraging people to keep our community clean

We should keep our community clean because...

_____

_____

Poster Checklist:

☐ My poster tells people to keep our community clean.

☐ My poster includes a picture.

☐ My poster is easy to read.

Where Does the Trash Go?

People make a lot of trash.
A truck picks the trash up.

Most trash goes to a landfill.
Machines dig dirt to cover
the trash.

This truck is picking up trash
to take to the landfill.

The landfill can get full.
When the landfull is full,
where will the trash go?
You can help by making less trash.

This machine is moving around trash in a landfill.

"Where Does the Trash Go?"—Think About It!

1. What is a landfill? How do you know?

_____

2. Write one fact you know about landfills.

_____

3. What does each picture show?

_____

4. What can you do to make less trash? Put a ✔.

   ☐ Use both sides of paper.

   ☐ Give clothes that do not fit you to smaller kids.

   ☐ Save leftover food for snacks.

5. Draw a picture of what you do to make less trash.

People in Our Community

Match the job to the correct community worker.

Teacher

Construction Worker

Postal Worker

Police Officer

Firefighter

Doctor

Utility Worker

Sanitation Worker

Dentist

My job is to keep people's teeth healthy.

My job is to protect people.

My job is to put out fires.

My job is to teach children.

My job is to make sure people have electricity.

My job is to keep the community clean.

My job is to build buildings.

My job is to deliver mail.

My job is to keep people healthy and to help sick people get better

A Community Worker

Write about a community worker.

Community worker _____

This worker helps the community by _____

_____ .

Name a special tool that this community worker uses.

_____

When I Grow Up...

When I grow up I want to be a _____

The reason is because _____

_____

_____

_____

Staying Safe Poster

Here are a few things to do that will help keep you safe.

1. Wear a helmet when you ride your bike.
2. Obey all traffic lights.
3. Look both ways when you walk across the street.
4. Always wear a seat belt in the car, even if you do not have far to go.
5. Do not play in the street, even if you do not see any cars. Cars can come up quickly.

Make a poster about staying safe.

"Staying Safe Poster"—Think About It!

1. What is the purpose of this poster?

_____

2. What should you wear when you ride a bike?

_____

3. Why should you look both ways when you walk across the street?

_____

_____

4. What is another way to stay safe when you walk across the street?

_____

_____

5. It is okay to not wear a seat belt if you do not have far to go. Circle the answer. **Yes   No**

6. It is okay to play in the street as long as you do not see any cars. Circle the answer. **Yes   No**

Help!

When something bad happens, there is a special number to call for help. We call this an emergency.

We can call the number if there is a fire.
We can call if someone is very sick or hurt.
We can call if someone is robbed.
We can call if someone needs help in a boat or on a mountain.

Draw a picture of someone being helped in an emergency.

"Help!"—Think About It!

1. What do you think of when you hear the word *help*?

_____

_____

2. Name two things that are used to put out a fire.

_____

_____

3. What kind of truck comes when people call about a fire?

_____

4. Do you know the special number to call in your area?

_____

5. Name three times people can call the special number.

_____

_____

_____

What Is a Smoke Detector?

A smoke detector tells you when there is smoke from something burning.

When there is smoke, a smoke detector starts to beep very loudly. This warns people that there may be a fire.

What should you do when a smoke detector is beeping loudly?

Here is what to do:

First, go outside.
Next, find an adult.
Finally, ask for help.

Draw what to do when a smoke detector beeps.

Write a sentence about your picture.

"What Is a Smoke Detector?"—Think About It!

1. What does a smoke detector do?

_____

2. What sound does it make?

_____

3. How does the checklist help you understand the text?

_____

4. If you hear a smoke detector, what do you do:

First, _____

Next, _____

Finally, _____

5. Circle True or False.

A smoke detector lets you
know when dinner is ready.   A. True   B. False

6. Circle True or False.

A smoke detector
beeps loudly.   A. True   B. False

Families Can Be Different

A family is made up of people who care about you.

Each family is different. Each family is special.

Some of us have a mom and dad.

Some of us only have a mom or a dad.

Some of us have stepparents.

Some of us have brothers or sisters.

Some of us have grandparents, aunts, uncles, and cousins.

Some of us have friends who take care of us like family.

Draw a picture of your family.

My family is special because...

_____

"Families Can Be Different"—Think About It!

1. How many people are in your family?

_____

2. Who are the people in your family?

_____

_____

3. Does everyone in your family live in the same home, or do some live somewhere else?

_____

_____

4. What is special about your family?

_____

_____

5. What kind of things do you like to do as a family?

_____

_____

_____

Families Work Together

Think of the ways you help out at home. Draw a picture.

List the ways you help out at home.

_____

_____

_____

_____

Growing Up

Is there a baby in your family?

Did you know you used to be as little as they are right now?

It is true!

But you have grown.

Next year you will be even bigger.

You will also be taller next year.

You will also know how to do more things.

Each year you will grow more and learn more.

What does this text remind you of? Draw a picture.

Write a sentence about your picture.

_____

"Growing Up"—Think About It!

1. Is there a baby in your family? How old is the baby?

_____

2. What do you like to do in school?

_____

_____

3. If you could be any age right now, how old would you want to be? Why?

_____

_____

_____

4. What does the text say you will be like next year?

_____

_____

5. When is your next birthday? How old will you be then?

_____

_____

How Have You Grown and Changed?

	When I was little	Now
My size		
The food I eat		
The toys I like		
Where I sleep		

Helping at Home

There are many ways you can help out at home.

You can make your bed.

You can put your clothes away.

You can keep you room neat.

You can help your family carry bags.

You can help set and clear the table.

It is good to help your family!

Draw a picture of how you help out at home.

Write a sentence about your picture.

"Helping at Home"—Think About It!

1. Name three things from the text that you can do to help at home.

_____

_____

_____

2. What can you do to keep your room neat?

_____

3. Do you like to help shop for food? Why?

_____

_____

4. Can you think of one more way to help out at home?

_____

_____

5. How could you help out if you had a pet at home?

_____

_____

Cleaning Your Room

What does your room look like?

Do you have a mess on your floor?

Do your mom and dad bug you to clean your room?

Here is how you can clean your room:

• Make your bed.

• Pick everything up off the floor.

• Throw out things you do not need.

• Fold your clothes and put them away.

It feels good to have a clean, neat room.

Draw a picture of you doing something to clean your room.

Write a sentence about your picture.

_____

"Cleaning Your Room"—Think About It!

1. Is your room neat? Circle the answer. **Yes**   **No**

2. Where do you keep your clothes?

_____

3. Name three things you can do to clean your room.

_____

_____

_____

4. Where can you put things that you do not need?

_____

5. Draw your room, as you would like it to look.

You Can Help with a Baby

A baby can be fun!

A baby might cry a lot.

You can talk or sing to the baby.

That might make them happy.

You can read them a story.

You can play a game with them.

It feels good to help out with a baby!

Draw a picture of you helping out with a baby.

Write a sentence about your picture.

"You Can Help with a Baby"—Think About It!

1. What do you think might make a baby cry?

_____

_____

2. What book would you like to read to a baby?

_____

3. What are some toys a baby might like to play with?

_____

_____

_____

4. Name one more way you can help with a baby.

_____

_____

5. What games do you think a baby would like to play?

_____

_____

_____

Are You Ready?

Does the alarm clock wake you up in the morning?

Or does your mom or dad tell you it is time to get up?

What do you do after you get out of bed?

Do you brush your teeth?

Do you get dressed?

Do you make your bed?

Do you comb your hair?

Do you eat breakfast?

That is how most kids start their day.

Draw a picture of you getting ready.

Write a sentence about your picture.

"Are You Ready?"—Think About It!

1. Name two of the ways people wake up in the morning.

_____

_____

2. What do you usually eat for breakfast before school?

_____

_____

3. Do you pick your own clothes for school? If so, what do you like to wear?

_____

_____

4. How many times a day do you brush your teeth?

_____

5. Name something else you do before you go to school.

_____

_____

What I Am Learning at School

Every day we learn something new at school.

We learn how to count.

We learn how to read.

We learn how to follow rules.

We learn how to be nice and to play with others.

We learn how to ask about things.

We learn how to listen to other people's ideas.

We learn about art and music.

Draw a picture of your favourite thing about school.

Write a sentence about you picture.

"What I Am Learning at School"—Think About It!

1. Name two things you learned at school this week.

_____

_____

2. Why is it important to be nice to others?

_____

_____

3. Why is it important to listen to other people?

_____

_____

4. What do you like to do at school?

_____

_____

5. List two rules at school and why they are important.

_____

_____

Thinking About Rules

What rules do you need to follow at home, or at school?

What is the rule?	Where do you have this rule?	What is the reason for this rule?

Living Things

All living things need air, water, and food.
All living things grow and change.

People are living things. 	Animals are living things. 	Plants are living things. 

Think About It!

1. What do all living things need?

_____

2. Is a squirrel a living thing? How do you know?

_____

_____

_____

3. Look at the pictures below. Circle the things that are living. Tell a partner how you know each thing is alive.

a) **toy car**

b) **teddy bear**

c) **man**

d) **dog**

e) **feather**

f) **piano stool**

g) **cow**

h) **flower**

Living Things Collage

Look for pictures of living things in magazines. Cut out the pictures and paste them below.

Write a sentence about living things.

_____

_____

Non-living Things Collage

Look for pictures of non-living things in magazines.
Cut out the pictures and paste them below.

Write a sentence about non-living things.

_____

_____

Draw a line from each label to the right part of the body.

hair

ear

nose

wrist

chin

arm

neck

chest

stomach

foot

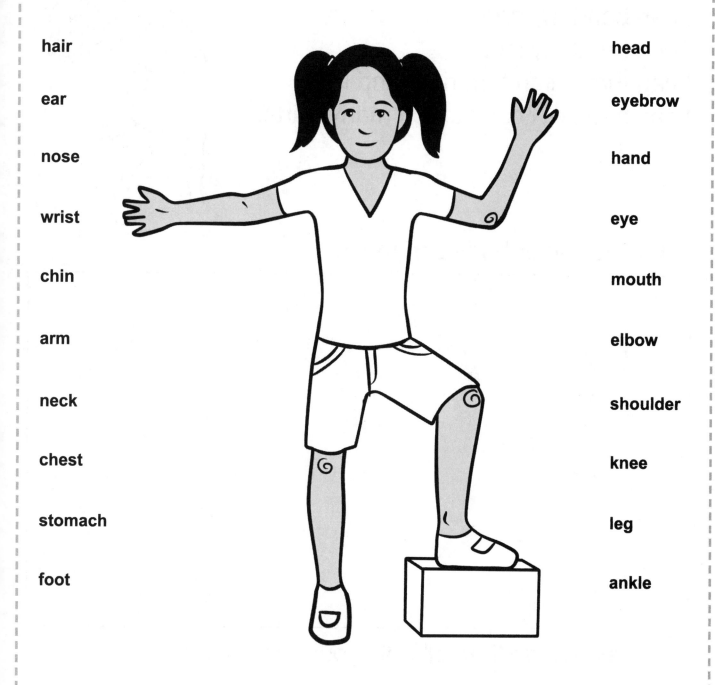

head

eyebrow

hand

eye

mouth

elbow

shoulder

knee

leg

ankle

I Can Move My Body

I can move my body in many ways.
I can bend. I can bend low.
I can bend my arm.
I can bend my leg.
I can turn. I can turn right and left.
I can stretch. I can stretch many parts.

Show how your body can move.

Write the words that tell how your body moves.

"I Can Move My Body"—Think About It!

1. Who do you think is telling the story? Explain.

_____

_____

2. What do the words *bend*, *turn*, and *stretch* describe?

_____

_____

3. How does the boy move his body in the picture?

_____

4. From the text, you can guess that the boy likes to move. Circle the correct answer.

A. TRUE

B. FALSE

Baby Teeth

Baby teeth do not stay forever. Baby teeth fall out so adult teeth can grow in.

Most children have 20 baby teeth when they are three years old.

When a baby tooth is ready to fall out, it moves. Sometimes children do not feel it when a tooth falls out.

After a baby tooth falls out, an adult tooth grows in.

Think About It!

1. Have any of your baby teeth fallen out? How many?

_____

2. What did it feel like when your baby tooth fell out?

_____

3. How many baby teeth do most children have at age 3?

_____

4. What grows in after a baby tooth falls out?

_____

5. What happens when a tooth is ready to fall out?

_____

Brush Your Teeth

Brushing your teeth is important for your body. Brushing helps you stay well.

Brush your teeth at least two times a day.

Brush your teeth in the morning and at night.

Brush your teeth after you eat foods that have sugar.

First, put toothpaste on your toothbrush.

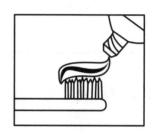

Next, pour a little water on your toothbrush.

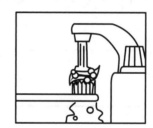

Then, make sure to brush all of your teeth.

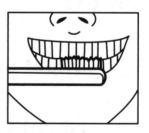

Last, rinse your mouth with water.

"Brush Your Teeth"—Think About It!

1. Why do you think it is important to brush your teeth?

_____

_____

2. How many times a day should you brush your teeth?

_____

3. Do you think you do a good job brushing your teeth?
Tell why or why not.

_____

_____

4. Number the steps in order for brushing your teeth.

_____ Make sure to brush all of your teeth.

_____ Rinse your mouth with water.

_____ Pour a little water on your toothbrush.

_____ Put toothpaste on your toothbrush.

Clean Hands

Germs can make you sick.

Soap kills germs.

Wash your hands with soap.

Clean hands keep germs away.

Wash your hands before eating.

Wash your hands after you go to the bathroom!

Think About It!

1. Fill in the blanks.

a) Germs can make you _____.

b) Wash your hands with _____.

c) Clean hands help keep _____ away.

d) Wash your hands before you _____.

e) Wash your hands after you go to the _____.

2. Do you agree it is important to wash your hands? Tell why or why not.

_____

Steps for Washing Hands

1. First, wet your hands under warm water.

2. Next, cover your hands with soap.

3. Then, scrub the soap all over your hands for 20 to 30 seconds.

4. After, rinse the soap off under warm water.

5. Finally, dry your hands.

Think About It!

Match each sentence to the correct step.

First	Rinse the soap off under warm water.
Next	Dry your hands.
Then	Cover your hands with soap.
After	Scrub the soap all over your hands for 20 to 30 seconds.
Finally	Wet your hands under warm water.

Cover Sneezes and Coughs

When you have a cold, you sneeze.

When you have a cold, you cough.

Coughing and sneezing spread germs.

Germs make people sick.

You can stop germs from spreading.

When you cough, cover your mouth.

When you sneeze, use a tissue.

If you do not have a tissue, cough or sneeze into your sleeve.

"Cover Sneezes and Coughs"—Think About It!

1. How does the title help you understand the text?

_____

_____

2. What happens when you sneeze or cough?

_____

_____

3. What do the pictures help you to learn?

_____

4. List two ways you can stop germs from spreading.

_____

_____

5. What is the author trying to teach the reader?

_____

6. What might you say when a friend sneezes?

_____

Growing Up

Is there a baby in your family?

Did you know you used to be as little as they are right now? It is true!

But you have grown. Next year you will be even bigger.

You will also be taller next year.

You will also know how to do more things.

Each year you will grow more and learn more.

"Growing Up"—Think About It!

1. If you could be any age right now, how old would you want to be? I would want to be age _____. Draw a picture.

2. Explain why you want to be that age.

_____

_____

_____

3. Complete the chart. How have you changed?

	When I was little	Now
My size		
The food I eat		
The toys I like to play with		
Where I sleep		

Using Braille to Read Without Seeing

People who are blind or who have trouble seeing sometimes read braille.

Braille is an alphabet made up of tiny bumps. People can use their fingers to read, instead of their eyes. They run their fingers across the bumps from left to right, just like you read.

Braille Alphabet

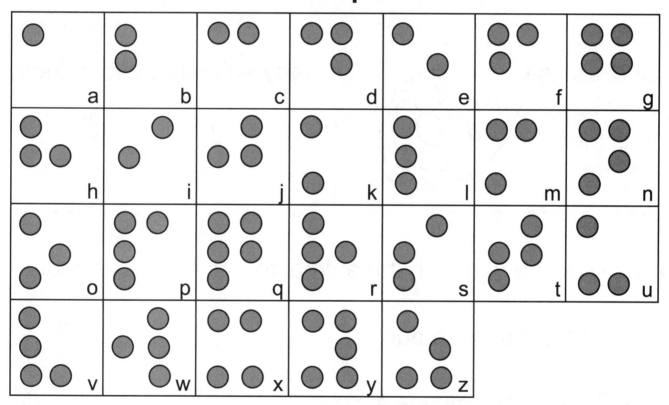

On a separate piece of paper, print your name in braille. Here is what you do:

1. Draw your name in dots. Use the braille alphabet above.

2. Put tiny bumps made of clay on the dots to make your name.

Animals On the Move

All animals have body parts to help them.
Animals move in different ways.

Fish have fins to help them swim.

Birds have wings to help them fly.

Snakes use their body to slither.

Many animals walk on legs.

1. Draw a line to match the animal to the way it can move.

a) This animal can hop.

b) This animal moves slowly.

c) This animal can move fast.

d) This animal can climb.

Comparing Living Things

Compare two living things. For example,

- Compare two animals.
- Compare two plants.
- Compare an animal to a human.

Comparing		
What is the size of it?		
What does it look like?		
How are they the same?		
How are they different?		

Needs of Living Things

Living things need air, food, and water.
Living things need a place to live.
Living things also need space to grow.

Animals and plants find what they need in their environment. This is the area where they live.

A pond is a home for cattails.

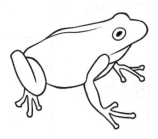

A pond is a home for frogs.

Brain Stretch

How does a chipmunk get what it needs to live?
(**Hint:** It needs food, air, and water, too.)

_____

_____

_____

chipmunk

About Seeds

A seed is a tiny plant waiting to grow.
A peanut is a seed.
A coconut is a seed.

Dandelion seeds have fluff on them.
Maple tree seeds have wings.

Sun, water, and soil help seeds
grow into plants.

Dandelions

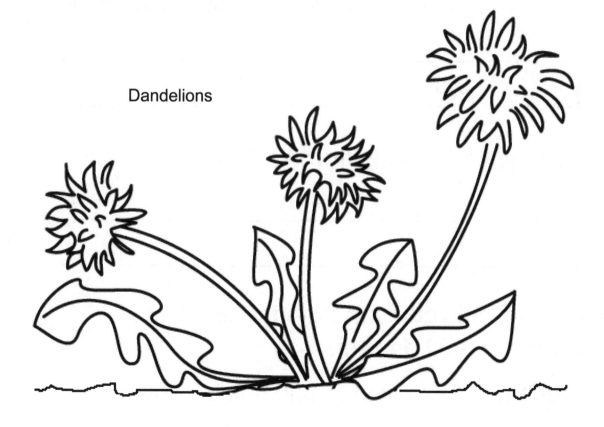

"About Seeds"—Think About It!

1. What does the text tell you a seed is?

_____

2. Name three things that help seeds to grow into plants.

_____

_____

_____

3. Some seeds have special parts that help them fly. Name the two special parts talked about in the text.

_____

_____

4. List two types of seeds from the text.

_____

_____

5. Which fact did you learn from the text? Circle the correct answer.

A. Seeds need sun, water, and soil to grow.

B. All seeds grow into plants that have flowers.

Animals Live in Different Places

1. Draw a line from the animal to where it lives.

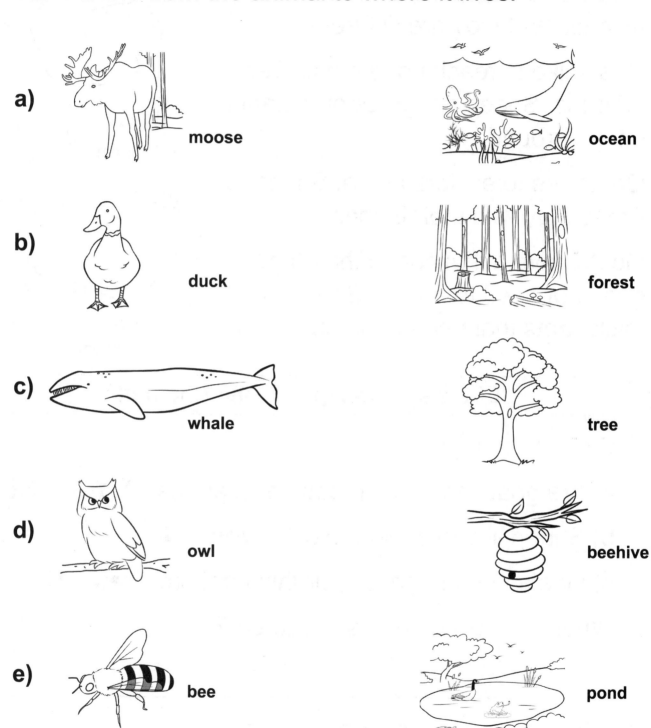

a) moose   ocean

b) duck   forest

c) whale   tree

d) owl   beehive

e) bee   pond

Goats and Sheep

Goats and sheep are both farm animals, but they are different.

Goats like to reach up to eat leaves off trees. Sheep eat grass and plants off the ground.

Goats like to explore alone. Sheep like to stay with their friends.

Goats have a thin coat of hair that does not need to be cut. Sheep grow thick coats that need to be cut.

goat

sheep

"Goats and Sheep"—Think About It!

1. Circle Yes or No.

a) Are goats and sheep both farm animals? **Yes   No**

b) Sheep like to explore alone. **Yes   No**

c) Goats need to have their thin coat cut. **Yes   No**

2. What and how do goats like to eat?

_____

3. What and how do sheep like to eat?

_____

A Healthy Environment

Animals and plants need a healthy environment.

What Animals Need Most	What Plants Need Most
• clean air • clean water • safe food to eat • shelter • space to grow	• clean air • clean water • sunlight to help make food • food in the soil to grow • space to grow

Think About It!

1. Draw and colour an animal. Show where it lives.
   Draw and label all the things it needs to live.

People Affect Living Things

Do	Do Not
Put garbage in a trash can	Put garbage in the water that living things drink and live in

| Walk on hiking trails in a park and look at wildflowers | Walk on plants or pick wildflowers |

"People Affect Living Things"—Think About It!

1. This picture shows polluted water. How might the pollution harm the fish that live in that water?

_____

2. Draw a way to help the environment.

[blank drawing box]

3. Write a sentence that tells about your picture.

_____

What Is Energy?

Energy makes things happen.

Energy makes us move.
Energy makes things work.

You need energy to run.

A video game needs energy to work.

Energy makes all living things grow.

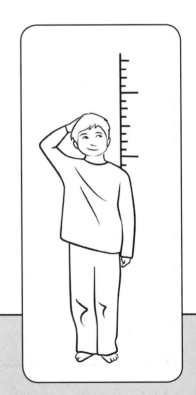

Brain Stretch

How do you get the energy you need to grow?

"What Is Energy?"—Think About It!

Complete each sentence. Use the words below.

energy   jump   create

1. You need energy to _____.

2. A plant needs _____ to grow.

3. A light bulb needs energy to _____ light.

4. Look at the pictures below.
   Circle the activities that use a lot of energy.

A.

B.

C.

D.

E.

F.

Where Energy Comes From

Energy comes from different sources.
A source is the place where something comes from.

Sun

gasoline

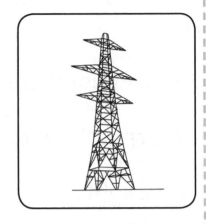

electricity

wind

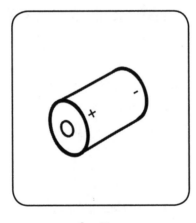

battery

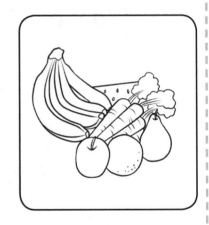

food

Think About It!

1. Colour each source of energy you use.
2. Tell a partner how you use each energy source.

We Get Energy From the Sun

The Sun is the main source of energy for all living things.

The Sun warms the air.
The Sun warms the land and water.

The Sun gives us light.
The Sun makes it possible to grow food.

Think About It!

1. Draw pictures to show three things that the Sun does.

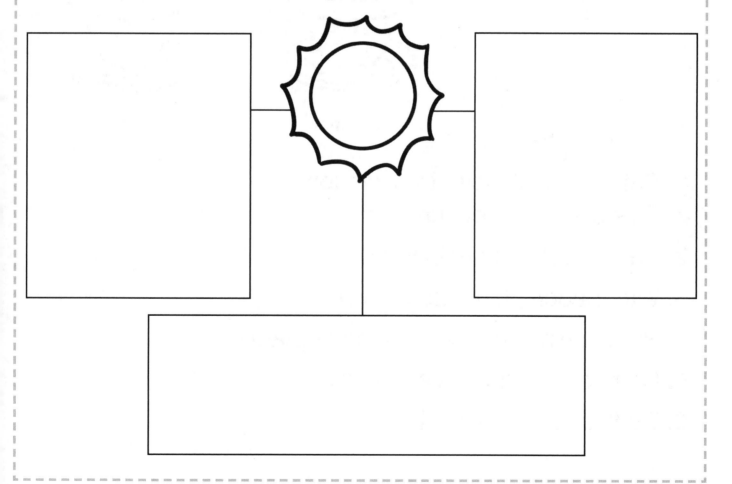

Experiment: How Does Sunlight Affect Plants?

The Sun gives us light.
Find out what effect sunlight has on plants.

What You Need

- 2 plants
- Water

sunlight   dark

What You Do

1. Put one plant close to a window.
   This plant will get sunlight.

2. Put the other plant in the dark.

3. Water each plant once a week.

4. Predict what will happen to the plants.

5. Compare the plants each week.

6. Do this for three weeks.

"Experiment: How Does Sunlight Affect Plants?"—Think About It!

1. What do you predict will happen?

_____

2. Draw a picture of each plant after three weeks.

Sunlight	**Dark**

3. Compare the pictures.
What happened to the plant that did not get sunlight?

_____

_____

4. What did you learn? Fill in the blank.

Plants need _____ to live and grow.

We Get Energy From Food

We need energy to do things.
We use energy to walk.
We even use energy to sleep.

All living things need energy to grow.
We get energy from food.

Look at the picture below.
The picture shows an energy chain.
Trace the flow of energy from the Sun.

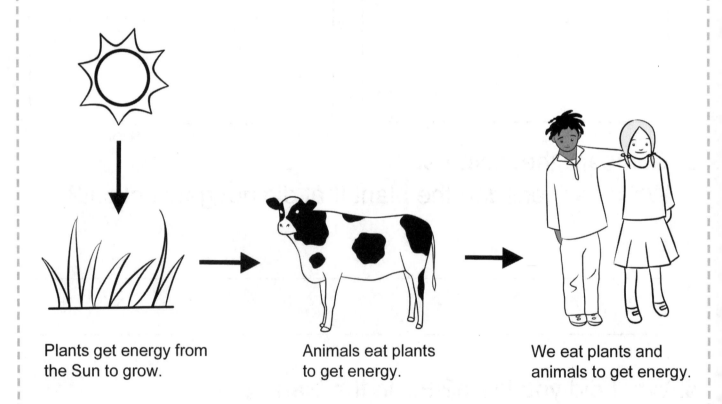

Plants get energy from
the Sun to grow.

Animals eat plants
to get energy.

We eat plants and
animals to get energy.

1. Label the diagram.

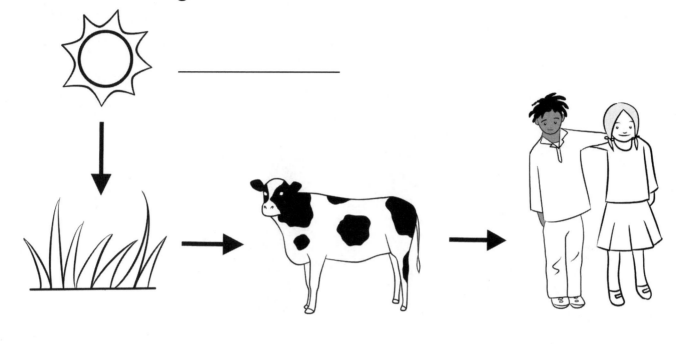

_____

_____   _____   _____

2. Complete each sentence. Use the words below.

energy   animals   plants   Sun

a) Plants get energy from the _____.

b) Some animals eat plants to get _____.

c) People eat _____ and

_____ to get energy.

Healthy Foods Collage

Cut and paste pictures of healthy foods.

Farmers

Farmers grow food. They sow seeds and care for plants. They pick fruits and vegetables.

Farmer picking apples

Farmers take care of animals. Chickens give eggs and meat. Cows give milk and meat.

Farmer taking care of her cows

Truck drivers take the food to stores.

Truck driver carrying vegetables

Store clerks sell the food.

Clerk selling food

"Farmers"—Think About It!

1. What do farmers grow?

_____

2. Where does meat come from?

_____

3. Who takes the food to the stores?

_____

4. Who sells you food?

_____

5. Draw a picture of your family cooking food together. Show what you are cooking.

Write a sentence about your picture.

_____

Energy at Work

Read how energy makes things work.

Electricity powers lights.

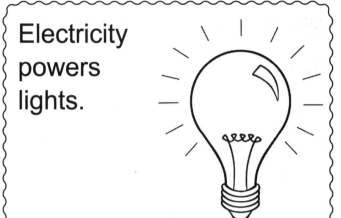

Wood, oil, and gas heat our homes.

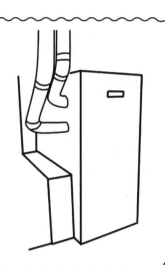

Gasoline makes cars and buses move.

Batteries power devices such as flashlights.

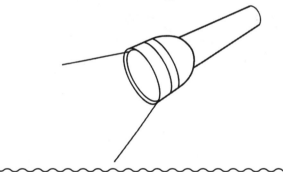

Brain Stretch

battery

List two different things that need batteries to work.

_____   _____

1. Write the source of energy for each item.
Use the words below.

battery   electricity   gasoline

Sun   wind   wood

a)

_____

b)

_____

c)

_____

d)

_____

e)

_____

f)

_____

Activity: Energy Matching Game

1. Draw a line to match the source of energy with where the energy is used. Write what kind of energy the source creates. Use the words below.

heat   **light**   **movement**   **sound**

wood

a)

kite

_____

electrical outlet

b)

campfire

_____

battery

c)

lamp

_____

wind

d)

radio

_____

Saving Energy

Here are some ways to save energy.

Turn off lights and electronics when you leave a room.

Do not hold the refrigerator door open.

Hang clothes on a line instead of using a dryer.

Walk to school instead of taking a ride.

Create a poster of tips for how to save energy. Use a separate piece of paper.

"Saving Energy"—Think About It!

1. Write **S** if the action saves energy.
Write **W** if the action wastes energy.

    a) Turn off the television when no one is watching. _____

    b) Turn on the dishwasher only when it is full. _____

    c) Use the washer to clean only your pyjamas. _____

    d) Open the curtains on a hot day. _____

    e) Hold the refrigerator door open until you decide what to eat. _____

2. Draw something that uses a lot of energy in your home. Label the item. Write a sentence about how you could use this item less.

_____

Objects Are Made From Materials

Objects are things we use.
Objects are made from one or more materials.

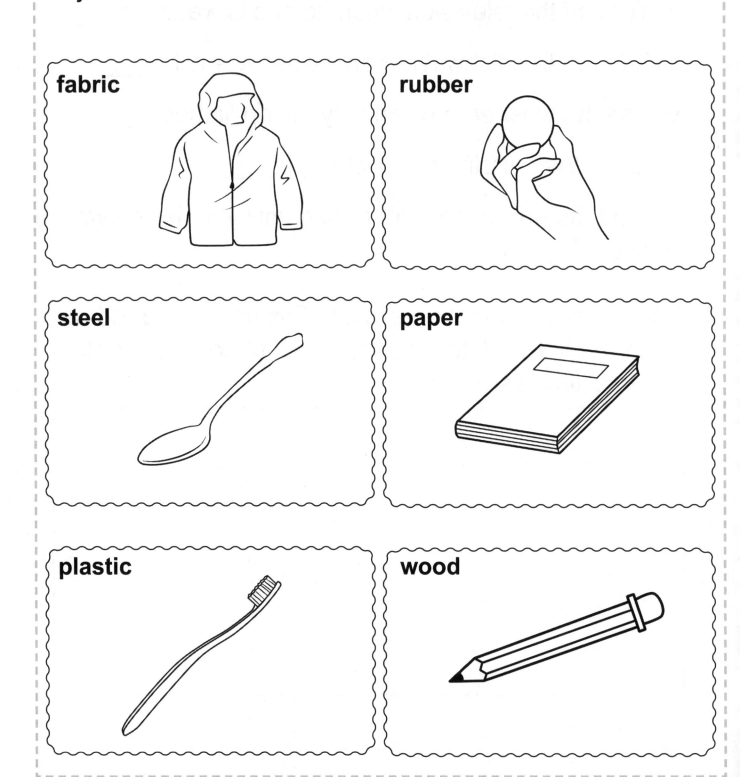

fabric

rubber

steel

paper

plastic

wood

"Objects Are Made From Materials"—Think About It!

1. Look in magazines for pictures of objects.
Find objects made from the materials below.
Cut out and paste one object for each material.

a) fabric

b) paper

c) plastic

d) rubber

e) steel

f) wood

2. Write a sentence about materials.

_____

Natural and Manufactured Materials

Some materials are found in nature.

Rubber is made from the sap of rubber trees.

Wood comes from trees.
Some trees are made into boards.
Other trees are used for paper.

Materials such as fabric are made by people.
These are called manufactured materials.

A beach pail is made from plastic.

Paper is made from tiny wood chips mixed with water.

1. Sort the words below into the right groups.
Print the words.

fabric   wool   plastic   tree sap   steel   wood

Natural Materials	Materials Made by People
_____	_____
_____	_____
_____	_____

Did You Know?

Some metals are natural.
These metals are found in rocks.
Metals such as steel are made by people.
Think of two other objects made from steel.

$1 coin

_____   _____

Where Do Materials Come From?

All materials made by people are made from natural things.

Paper is made from wood.

Rubber is made from tree sap.

Plastic is made from oil.

Steel is made from metals and minerals in rocks.

Fabric is made from natural materials.

Cotton comes from cotton plants.

Wool comes from sheep.

Think About It!

1. Draw a line from the material to what it is made from.

wool

paper

rubber

steel

fabric

 **tree sap**

 cotton

 rock

 tree

 sheep

Light and Heat Affect What We Do

The Sun is our main source of light and heat.
Sometimes, what we do depends on sunlight and heat.
On sunny days, the air is usually warmer.

swim

hike

play

On most nights, there is very little light and less heat.

sleep

watch the stars

watch fireworks

What Is It Like Outside?

There are different kinds of weather.
Temperature tells you how warm or cold it is outside.

1. Match the item you might use with the kind of weather.

The weather is sunny.

The weather is rainy.

The weather is snowy.

The weather is windy.

The weather is cool.

Brain Stretch

Circle the item that is used in hot weather.
Draw a square around the item that is
used in cold weather.

2. What will it be like outside when you wear these kinds of clothing? Use the words below.

hot
warm
cool
cold

hot   **warm**   **cool**   **cold**

a)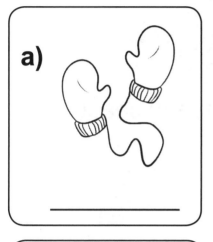

_____

b)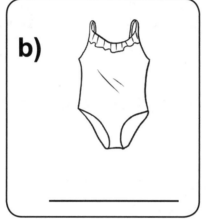

_____

c)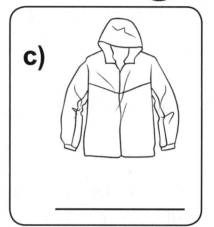

_____

d)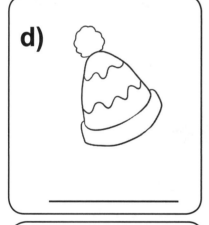

_____

e)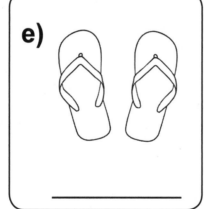

_____

f)

_____

g)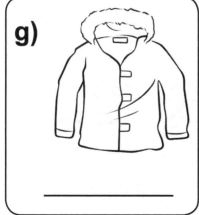

_____

h)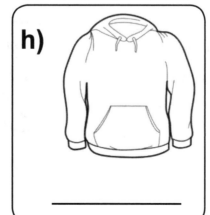

_____

i)

_____

The Seasons Affect What We Do

Some outdoor activities can only be done in certain seasons.

You can go sledding only in winter.

Some outdoor activities can be done in any season.

You can skate and play hockey in an arena. Arenas can create ice in all seasons.

You can swim at a community centre in all seasons.

Farmers can grow food in winter. They use a greenhouse to grow plants in cold weather.

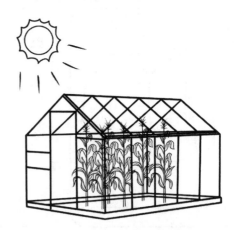

"The Seasons Affect What We Do"—Think About It!

1. Write the season in which each activity can be done. Use each word once.

spring   summer   fall   winter

a)

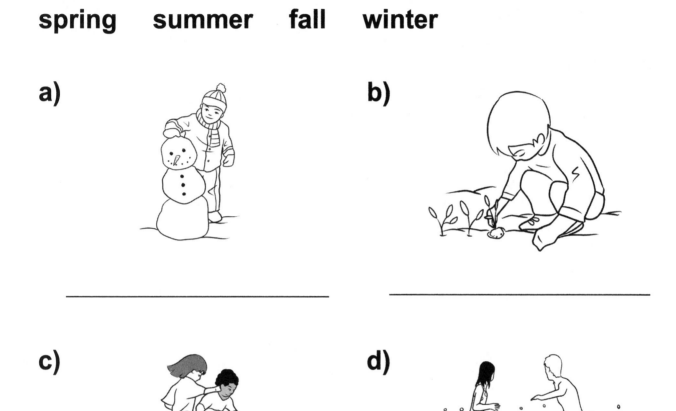

_____

b)

_____

c)

_____

d)

_____

2. Circle the activity that can be done in only one season.

3. How could one activity be done in a different season?

_____

My Favourite Season

Draw a picture of something you like to do during your favourite season.

My favourite season is _____.

Here are three reasons why I like this season best.

_____

_____

_____

Crazy Colouring Ideas

Have children practice their fine motor skills using different media to colour colouring pages or simple geometric shapes.

Colour a colouring page or large geometric shapes:

- on different surfaces such as sandpaper to create interesting textures

- alternating heavy and light strokes

- using only primary colours

- using only secondary colours

- using different shades of the same colour

- with different colours of chalk and setting it with hair spray

- using pastels

- using watercolours

- vertical lines

- horizontal lines

Fill in sections of a colouring page or geometric shape using:

- different colours of modelling clay

- tiny bits of torn construction paper

- mixed media

- different colours of thick yarn

- different patterns

- cotton swab dots

How to Draw a Seal

Follow these steps to draw. Write an adventure story about the seal.

Use an eraser to remove overlapping lines.

How to Draw an Elephant

Follow these steps to draw. Write an adventure story about the elephant.

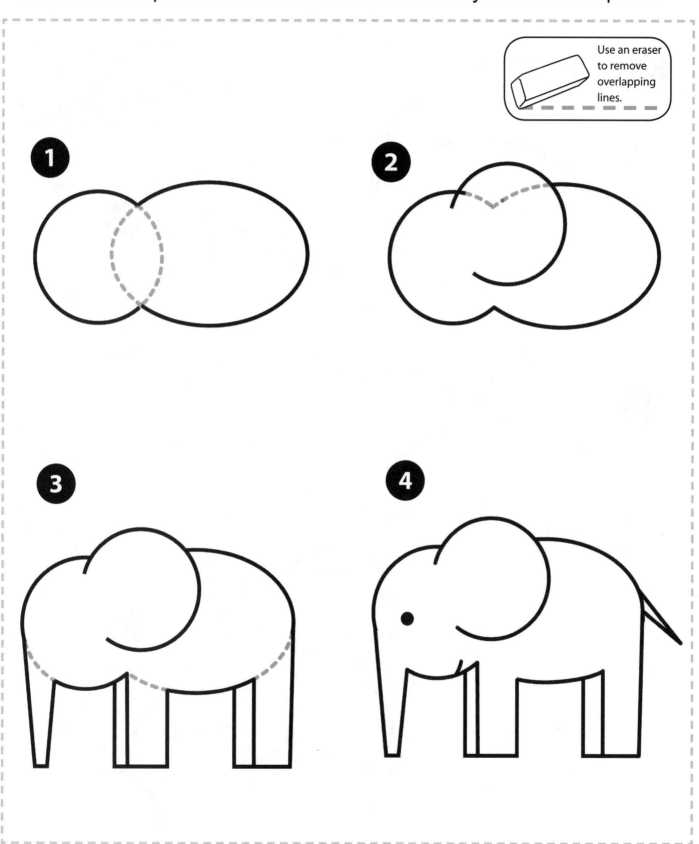

Use an eraser to remove overlapping lines.

How to Draw a Dolphin

Follow these steps to draw. Write an adventure story about the dolphin.

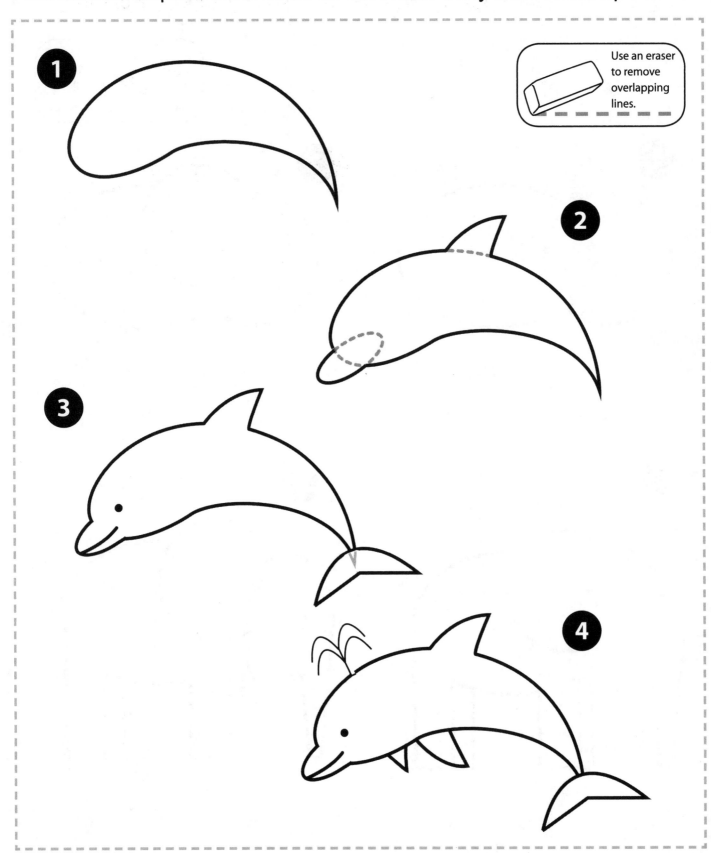

Use an eraser to remove overlapping lines.

How to Draw a Castle

Follow these steps to draw. Write an adventure story about the castle.

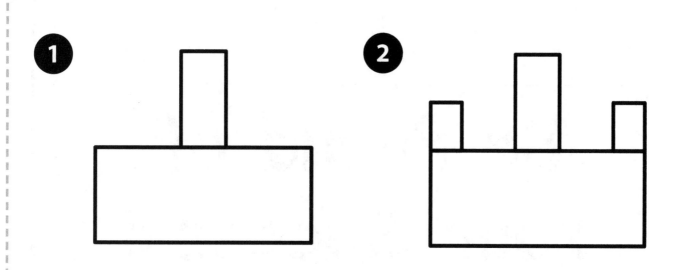

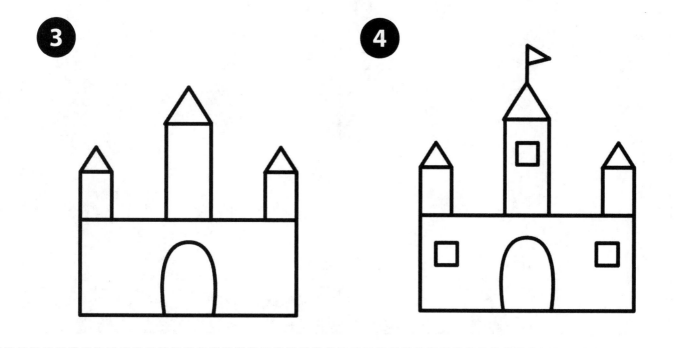

Fantastic Work!

Be Proud of Your Success!

Answers

Mathematics

Number Words

1. Trace the numbers and the number words.
   Draw a line to match the numbers to the counters.

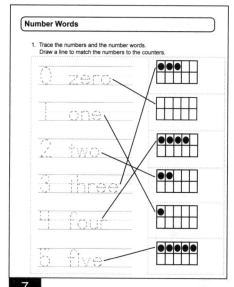

7

Number Words (continued)

2. Trace the numbers and the number words.
   Draw a line to match the numbers to the counters.

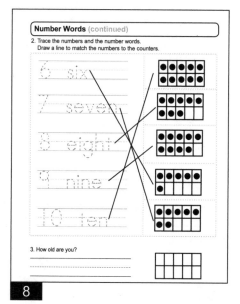

3. How old are you?

8

Numbers

1. Trace the numbers. Draw ●s to show each number.

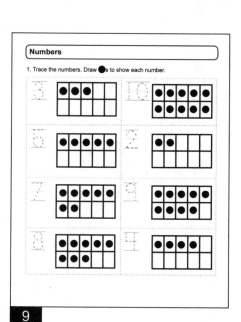

9

Using Ten-Frames to Count to 10

1. How many counters are there?

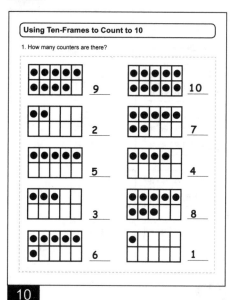

- 9
- 10
- 2
- 7
- 5
- 4
- 3
- 8
- 6
- 1

10

Comparing Numbers from 1 to 10

Compare numbers by counting.

3 is less than 5   4 is greater than 2   9 is equal to 9

1. Compare the numbers. Write the words **greater than**, **less than**, or **equal to**.

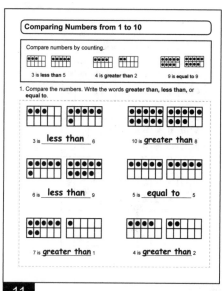

3 is **less than** 6   10 is **greater than** 8

6 is **less than** 9   5 is **equal to** 5

7 is **greater than** 1   4 is **greater than** 2

11

Numbers and Number Words

1. Draw a line from the number to the number word.

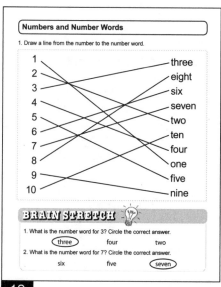

1 — three
2 — eight
3 — six
4 — seven
5 — two
6 — ten
7 — four
8 — one
9 — five
10 — nine

BRAIN STRETCH

1. What is the number word for 3? Circle the correct answer.

(three)   four   two

2. What is the number word for 7? Circle the correct answer.

six   five   (seven)

12

Number Words Word Search

1. Circle the correct words in the word search. Cross words off the list when you find them.

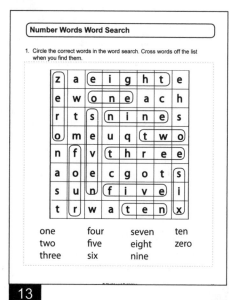

one   four   seven   ten
two   five   eight   zero
three   six   nine

13

Counting, Then Writing the Number

1. Look at the picture. How many of each creature? Write the number in the box below the creature.

| 10 | 4 | 7 | 6 | 5 |

14

More, Fewer, and Less

1. Circle the correct set. Write **more** or **fewer**.

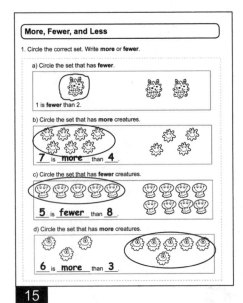

a) Circle the set that has **fewer**.

1 is **fewer** than 2.

b) Circle the set that has **more** creatures.

7 is **more** than **4**.

c) Circle the set that has **fewer** creatures.

5 is **fewer** than **8**.

d) Circle the set that has **more** creatures.

6 is **more** than **3**.

`15`

More, Fewer, and Less (continued)

2. Draw to show more or fewer shapes.

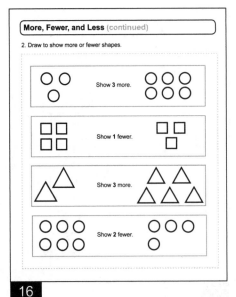

Show **3** more.

Show **1** fewer.

Show **3** more.

Show **2** fewer.

`16`

Using Ten-Frames to Count to 20

1. How many counters are there?

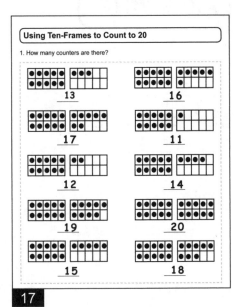

13   16

17   11

12   14

19   20

15   18

`17`

Using Ten-Frames to Count to 20 (continued)

2. Draw ●s in the ten-frames to equal the number.

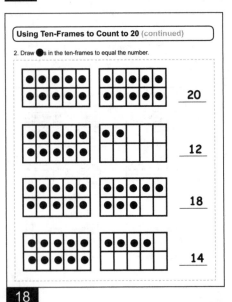

20

12

18

14

`18`

Using Ten-Frames to Count to 20 (continued)

3. Draw ●s in the ten-frames to equal the number.

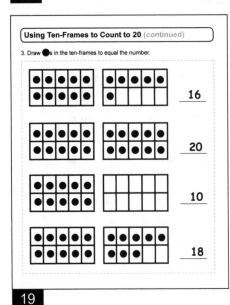

16

20

10

18

`19`

Using Ten-Frames to Count to 20 (continued)

4. Draw ●s in the ten-frames to equal the number.

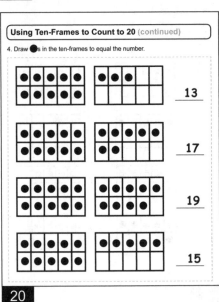

13

17

19

15

`20`

Skip Counting by 2s to 30

Connect the dots by skip counting by 2s from 0 to 30. Count out loud.

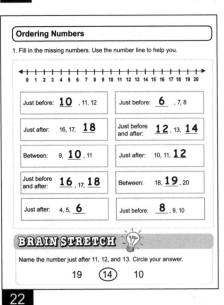

1. Give the creature a name. _____

2. What makes the creature special? _____

`21`

Ordering Numbers

1. Fill in the missing numbers. Use the number line to help you.

0 1 2 3 4 5 6 7 8 9 10 11 12 13 14 15 16 17 18 19 20

Just before: **10** , 11, 12

Just before: **6** , 7, 8

Just after: 16, 17, **18**

Just before and after: **12** , 13, **14**

Between: 9, **10** , 11

Just after: 10, 11, **12**

Just before and after: **16** , 17, **18**

Between: 18, **19** , 20

Just after: 4, 5, **6**

Just before: **8** , 9, 10

BRAIN STRETCH

Name the number just after 11, 12, and 13. Circle your answer.

19   (14)   10

`22`

Skip Counting by 5s to 100

Connect the dots by skip counting by 5s to 100. Count out loud.

1. Give the creature a name. _____

2. What makes the creature special? _____

`23`

Counting to 100

1. Fill in the missing numbers on the chart.

1	2	3	4	5	6	7	8	9	10
11	12	13	14	15	16	17	18	19	20
21	22	23	24	25	26	27	28	29	30
31	32	33	34	35	36	37	38	39	40
41	42	43	44	45	46	47	48	49	50
51	52	53	54	55	56	57	58	59	60
61	62	63	64	65	66	67	68	69	70
71	72	73	74	75	76	77	78	79	80
81	82	83	84	85	86	87	88	89	90
91	92	93	94	95	96	97	98	99	100

BRAIN STRETCH

How many legs do 1 chicken and one horse have in all? Show your thinking.

$2 + 4 = 6$

24

Skip Counting by 10s to 100

Connect the dots by skip counting by 10s to 100. Count out loud.

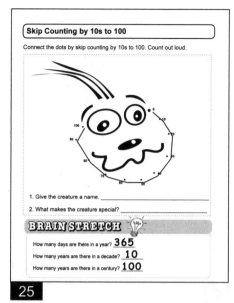

1. Give the creature a name. _____

2. What makes the creature special? _____

BRAIN STRETCH

How many days are there in a year? **365**

How many years are there in a decade? **10**

How many years are there in a century? **100**

25

Ordinal Numbers to 10

An ordinal number tells the position of something in a list.

1. Read the ordinal numbers. Underline the part that is the same.

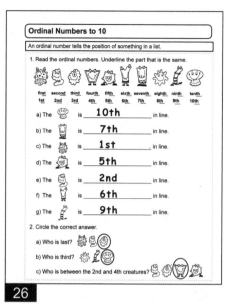

| first | second | third | fourth | fifth | sixth | seventh | eighth | ninth | tenth |
| 1st | 2nd | 3rd | 4th | 5th | 6th | 7th | 8th | 9th | 10th |

a) The ____ is **10th** in line.

b) The ____ is **7th** in line.

c) The ____ is **1st** in line.

d) The ____ is **5th** in line.

e) The ____ is **2nd** in line.

f) The ____ is **6th** in line.

g) The ____ is **9th** in line.

2. Circle the correct answer.

a) Who is last?

b) Who is third?

c) Who is between the 2nd and 4th creatures?

26

Groups of Ten

Circle the groups of ten. Count the ones left over. How many in all?

1. How many groups of 10? **2** How many left over? **1** How many in all? **21**

2. How many groups of 10? **1** How many left over? **5** How many in all? **15**

3. How many groups of 10? **2** How many left over? **6** How many in all? **26**

27

Groups of Ten (continued)

Circle the groups of ten. Count the ones left over. How many in all?

4. How many groups of 10? **1** How many left over? **6** How many in all? **16**

5. How many groups of 10? **2** How many left over? **9** How many in all? **29**

6. How many groups of 10? **3** How many left over? **1** How many in all? **31**

28

Tens and Ones

Count the tens and ones. Write how many blocks in all.

Each stack has **10** blocks.   Each block is one.

1 ten   + 3 ones   = 13 ones

1. **2** tens + **5** ones = **25** ones

2. **3** tens + **3** ones = **33** ones

3. **2** tens + **0** ones = **20** ones

4. **4** tens + **1** one = **41** ones

29

Tens and Ones (continued)

Count the tens and ones. Write how many blocks in all.

5. **5** tens + **4** ones = **54** ones

6. **2** tens + **7** ones = **27** ones

7. **3** tens + **5** ones = **35** ones

8. **1** ten + **8** ones = **18** ones

BRAIN STRETCH

Draw the blocks for 2 tens and 3 ones. What is the number?

23

30

Sums to 5

1. Use the blocks to complete the addition sentences.

1 + 3 = **4**
  plus   equals   sum

4 + 1 = **5**

1 + 2 = **3**

3 + 1 = **4**

2 + 1 = **3**

1 + 4 = **5**

3 + 2 = **5**

1 + 1 = **2**

2 + 2 = **4**

2 + 3 = **5**

31

Sums to 5 (continued)

2. Draw ●s to help you add.

3 + 2 = **5**

1 + 2 = **3**

4 + 1 = **5**

2 + 2 = **4**

1 + 1 = **2**

1 + 3 = **4**

2 + 3 = **5**

3 + 1 = **4**

1 + 4 = **5**

2 + 1 = **3**

32

Sums to 5 (continued)

3. Use the key to colour the picture.

Colour Key
1 – yellow
2 – orange
3 – green
4 – blue
5 – red

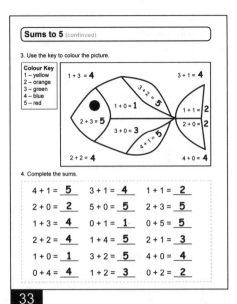

$1 + 3 = 4$ $3 + 1 = 4$
$3 + 2 = 5$
$1 + 0 = 1$ $1 + 1 = 2$
$2 + 3 = 5$ $2 + 0 = 2$
$3 + 0 = 3$
$2 + 2 = 4$ $4 + 1 = 5$ $4 + 0 = 4$

4. Complete the sums.

$4 + 1 = 5$	$3 + 1 = 4$	$1 + 1 = 2$
$2 + 0 = 2$	$5 + 0 = 5$	$2 + 3 = 5$
$1 + 3 = 4$	$0 + 1 = 1$	$0 + 5 = 5$
$2 + 2 = 4$	$1 + 4 = 5$	$2 + 1 = 3$
$1 + 0 = 1$	$3 + 2 = 5$	$4 + 0 = 4$
$0 + 4 = 4$	$1 + 2 = 3$	$0 + 2 = 2$

33

Addition Facts for 2, 3, 4, and 5

1. Use the key to colour the picture.

Colour Key
2 – red
3 – blue
4 – green
5 – yellow

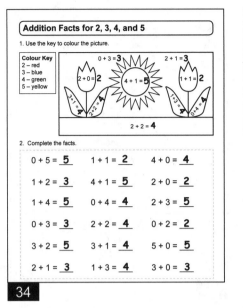

$0 + 3 = 3$ $2 + 1 = 3$
$2 + 0 = 2$ $4 + 1 = 5$ $1 + 1 = 2$
$3 + 1 = 4$ $2 + 2 = 4$ $1 + 3 = 4$ $0 + 4 = 4$
$2 + 2 = 4$

2. Complete the facts.

$0 + 5 = 5$	$1 + 1 = 2$	$4 + 0 = 4$
$1 + 2 = 3$	$4 + 1 = 5$	$2 + 0 = 2$
$1 + 4 = 5$	$0 + 4 = 4$	$2 + 3 = 5$
$0 + 3 = 3$	$2 + 2 = 4$	$0 + 2 = 2$
$3 + 2 = 5$	$3 + 1 = 4$	$5 + 0 = 5$
$2 + 1 = 3$	$1 + 3 = 4$	$3 + 0 = 3$

34

Addition Facts for 6, 7, 8, and 9

1. Use the key to colour the picture.

Colour Key
6 – red
7 – blue
8 – green
9 – yellow

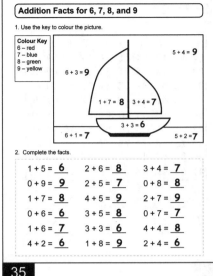

$5 + 4 = 9$
$6 + 3 = 9$
$1 + 7 = 8$ $3 + 4 = 7$
$3 + 3 = 6$
$6 + 1 = 7$ $5 + 2 = 7$

2. Complete the facts.

$1 + 5 = 6$	$2 + 6 = 8$	$3 + 4 = 7$
$0 + 9 = 9$	$2 + 5 = 7$	$0 + 8 = 8$
$1 + 7 = 8$	$4 + 5 = 9$	$2 + 7 = 9$
$0 + 6 = 6$	$3 + 5 = 8$	$0 + 7 = 7$
$1 + 6 = 7$	$3 + 3 = 6$	$4 + 4 = 8$
$4 + 2 = 6$	$1 + 8 = 9$	$2 + 4 = 6$

35

How Many Ways Can You Make 10?

Use the ten-frames to make 10. Use two different colours. Then, write the answers.

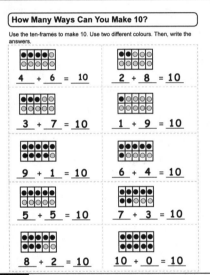

$4 + 6 = 10$ $2 + 8 = 10$
$3 + 7 = 10$ $1 + 9 = 10$
$9 + 1 = 10$ $6 + 4 = 10$
$5 + 5 = 10$ $7 + 3 = 10$
$8 + 2 = 10$ $10 + 0 = 10$

36

Addition Practice—Sums Up to 10

1. Write the number sentence.

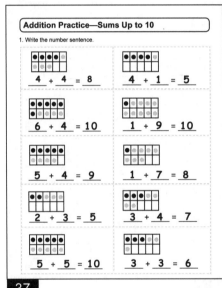

$4 + 4 = 8$ $4 + 1 = 5$
$6 + 4 = 10$ $1 + 9 = 10$
$5 + 4 = 9$ $1 + 7 = 8$
$2 + 3 = 5$ $3 + 4 = 7$
$5 + 5 = 10$ $3 + 3 = 6$

37

Addition Practice—Sums Up to 10 (continued)

2. Write the number sentence.

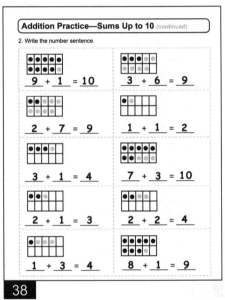

$9 + 1 = 10$ $3 + 6 = 9$
$2 + 7 = 9$ $1 + 1 = 2$
$3 + 1 = 4$ $7 + 3 = 10$
$2 + 1 = 3$ $2 + 2 = 4$
$1 + 3 = 4$ $8 + 1 = 9$

38

Adding 1 or 2 by Counting On

Add 1 by counting on.	**Add 2 by counting on.**
$4 + 1 =$ ___	$4 + 2 =$ ___
Start with the greater number.	Start with the greater number.
Count on by 1.	Count on by 2
4 5	4 5 6
Stop when 1 finger is up.	Stop when 2 fingers are up.
$4 + 1 = 5$	$4 + 2 = 6$

1. Count on to add.

$7 + 1 = 8$ $3 + 2 = 5$
7, 8 3, 4, 5

$1 + 1 = 2$ $8 + 2 = 10$
1, 2 8, 9, 10

$6 + 1 = 7$ $2 + 2 = 4$
6, 7 2, 3, 4

$5 + 1 = 6$ $5 + 2 = 7$
5, 6 5, 6, 7

39

Adding 1 or 2 by Counting On (continued)

2. Count on to add.

$9 + 1 = 10$ $0 + 2 = 2$
9, 10 0, 1, 2

$8 + 1 = 9$ $7 + 2 = 9$
8, 9 7, 8, 9

$4 + 1 = 5$ $9 + 2 = 11$
4, 5 9, 10, 11

$0 + 1 = 1$ $5 + 2 = 7$
0, 1 5, 6, 7

$6 + 1 = 7$ $1 + 2 = 3$
6, 7 1, 2, 3

$2 + 1 = 3$ $4 + 2 = 6$
2, 3 4, 5, 6

40

Using a Number Line to Add

Use a number line to add.

$6 + 3 = 9$

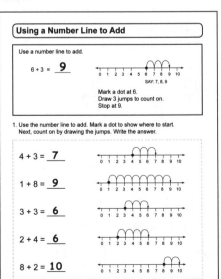

SAY: 7, 8, 9

Mark a dot at 6.
Draw 3 jumps to count on.
Stop at 9.

1. Use the number line to add. Mark a dot to show where to start. Next, count on by drawing the jumps. Write the answer.

$4 + 3 = 7$

$1 + 8 = 9$

$3 + 3 = 6$

$2 + 4 = 6$

$8 + 2 = 10$

41

Using a Number Line to Add (continued)

2. Use the number line to add by counting on. Mark a dot to show where to start. Next, draw the jumps. Write the answer.

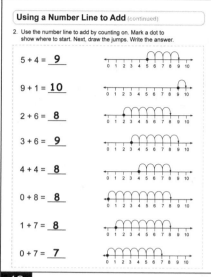

5 + 4 = __9__

9 + 1 = __10__

2 + 6 = __8__

3 + 6 = __9__

4 + 4 = __8__

0 + 8 = __8__

1 + 7 = __8__

0 + 7 = __7__

42

Making Addition Sentences

1. Show three ways to make each number. Use two colours to colour the blocks.

Sample answers:

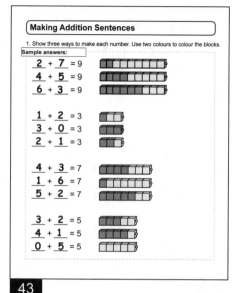

__2__ + __7__ = 9
__4__ + __5__ = 9
__6__ + __3__ = 9

__1__ + __2__ = 3
__3__ + __0__ = 3
__2__ + __1__ = 3

__4__ + __3__ = 7
__1__ + __6__ = 7
__5__ + __2__ = 7

__3__ + __2__ = 5
__4__ + __1__ = 5
__0__ + __5__ = 5

43

Making Addition Sentences (continued)

2. Show three ways to make each number. Use two colours to colour the blocks.

Sample answers:

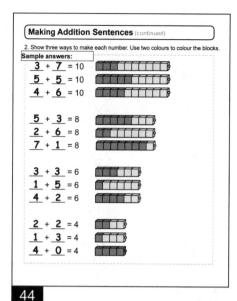

__3__ + __7__ = 10
__5__ + __5__ = 10
__4__ + __6__ = 10

__5__ + __3__ = 8
__2__ + __6__ = 8
__7__ + __1__ = 8

__3__ + __3__ = 6
__1__ + __5__ = 6
__4__ + __2__ = 6

__2__ + __2__ = 4
__1__ + __3__ = 4
__4__ + __0__ = 4

44

Addition Facts to 10

1. Draw a line from the number sentence to the correct answer.

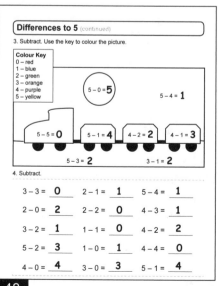

5 + 3 =   3   1 + 2 =
2 + 3 =   8   8 + 1 =
6 + 3 =   1   2 + 5 =
1 + 1 =   10   0 + 2 =
3 + 0 =   2   1 + 4 =
5 + 5 =   9   0 + 1 =
1 + 0 =   5   1 + 3 =
4 + 3 =   4   2 + 4 =
3 + 3 =   6   3 + 7 =
2 + 2 =   7   4 + 4 =

BRAIN STRETCH

4 + 1 + 5 = **10**   7 + 2 + 1 = **10**

45

Differences to 5

1. Count the blocks, then cross them out to finish the subtraction number sentences.

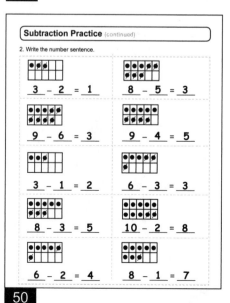

3 − 1 = __2__
    ↑minus ↑equals ↑difference

5 − 4 = __1__

4 − 1 = __3__

2 − 1 = __1__

4 − 2 = __2__

5 − 2 = __3__

5 − 3 = __2__

5 − 1 = __4__

4 − 3 = __1__

3 − 2 = __1__

46

Differences to 5 (continued)

2. Draw ● s, then cross them out to help you subtract.

5 − 2 = __3__

1 − 1 = __0__

3 − 2 = __1__

5 − 1 = __4__

4 − 3 = __1__

3 − 1 = __2__

5 − 4 = __1__

4 − 2 = __2__

5 − 3 = __2__

4 − 1 = __3__

47

Differences to 5 (continued)

3. Subtract. Use the key to colour the picture.

Colour Key
0 – red
1 – blue
2 – green
3 – orange
4 – purple
5 – yellow

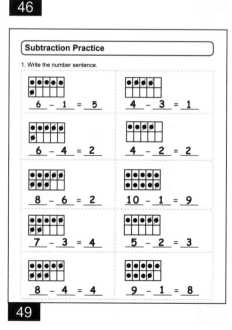

5 − 0 = **5**

5 − 4 = 1

5 − 5 = **0**

5 − 1 = **4**

4 − 2 = **2**

4 − 1 = **3**

5 − 3 = **2**

3 − 1 = **2**

4. Subtract.

3 − 3 = **0**   2 − 1 = **1**   5 − 4 = **1**

2 − 0 = **2**   2 − 2 = **0**   4 − 3 = **1**

3 − 2 = **1**   1 − 1 = **0**   4 − 2 = **2**

5 − 2 = **3**   1 − 0 = **1**   4 − 4 = **0**

4 − 0 = **4**   3 − 0 = **3**   5 − 1 = **4**

48

Subtraction Practice

1. Write the number sentence.

__6__ − __1__ = __5__

__4__ − __3__ = __1__

__6__ − __4__ = __2__

__4__ − __2__ = __2__

__8__ − __6__ = __2__

__10__ − __1__ = __9__

__7__ − __3__ = __4__

__5__ − __2__ = __3__

__8__ − __4__ = __4__

__9__ − __1__ = __8__

49

Subtraction Practice (continued)

2. Write the number sentence.

__3__ − __2__ = __1__

__8__ − __5__ = __3__

__9__ − __6__ = __3__

__9__ − __4__ = __5__

__3__ − __1__ = __2__

__6__ − __3__ = __3__

__8__ − __3__ = __5__

__10__ − __2__ = __8__

__6__ − __2__ = __4__

__8__ − __1__ = __7__

50

How Many Ways Can You Subtract from 10?

1. Use the ten frames to show different ways to subtract from 10.

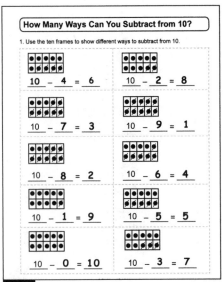

$10 - \underline{4} = 6$ $10 - \underline{2} = 8$

$10 - \underline{7} = 3$ $10 - \underline{9} = 1$

$10 - \underline{8} = 2$ $10 - \underline{6} = 4$

$10 - \underline{1} = 9$ $10 - \underline{5} = 5$

$10 - \underline{0} = 10$ $10 - \underline{3} = 7$

51

Subtracting 1 or 2 by Counting Back

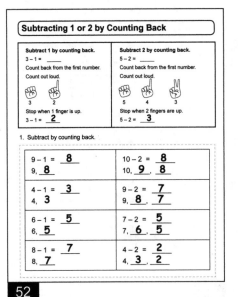

Subtract 1 by counting back.
$3 - 1 = $ _____
Count back from the first number.
Count out loud.

3 2

Stop when 1 finger is up.
$3 - 1 = \underline{2}$

Subtract 2 by counting back.
$5 - 2 = $ _____
Count back from the first number.
Count out loud.

5 4 3

Stop when 2 fingers are up.
$5 - 2 = \underline{3}$

1. Subtract by counting back.

$9 - 1 = \underline{8}$ 9, $\underline{8}$	$10 - 2 = \underline{8}$ 10, $\underline{9}$, $\underline{8}$
$4 - 1 = \underline{3}$ 4, $\underline{3}$	$9 - 2 = \underline{7}$ 9, $\underline{8}$, $\underline{7}$
$6 - 1 = \underline{5}$ 6, $\underline{5}$	$7 - 2 = \underline{5}$ 7, $\underline{6}$, $\underline{5}$
$8 - 1 = \underline{7}$ 8, $\underline{7}$	$4 - 2 = \underline{2}$ 4, $\underline{3}$, $\underline{2}$

52

Using a Number Line to Subtract

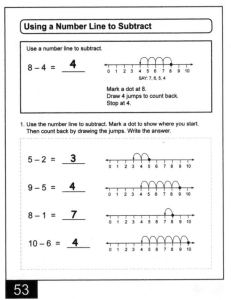

Use a number line to subtract.

$8 - 4 = \underline{4}$

SAY: 7, 6, 5, 4

Mark a dot at 8.
Draw 4 jumps to count back.
Stop at 4.

1. Use the number line to subtract. Mark a dot to show where you start. Then count back by drawing the jumps. Write the answer.

$5 - 2 = \underline{3}$

$9 - 5 = \underline{4}$

$8 - 1 = \underline{7}$

$10 - 6 = \underline{4}$

53

Using a Number Line to Subtract (continued)

2. Use the number line to subtract. Mark a dot to show where you start. Then count back by drawing the jumps. Write the answer.

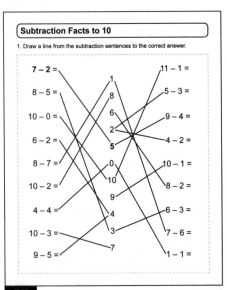

$7 - 2 = \underline{5}$

$6 - 4 = \underline{2}$

$3 - 3 = \underline{0}$

$4 - 1 = \underline{3}$

$9 - 7 = \underline{2}$

$7 - 5 = \underline{2}$

$10 - 8 = \underline{2}$

54

Making Subtraction Sentences

1. Cross out the blocks you want to take away. Colour the blocks left. Complete the subtraction sentence.

Sample answers:

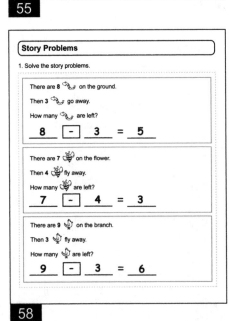

$4 - \underline{3} = 1$

$4 - \underline{2} = 2$

$4 - \underline{1} = 3$

$8 - \underline{4} = 4$

$8 - \underline{6} = 2$

$8 - \underline{3} = 5$

$5 - \underline{1} = 4$

$5 - \underline{3} = 2$

$5 - \underline{2} = 3$

55

Making Subtraction Sentences (continued)

2. Cross out the blocks you want to take away. Colour the blocks left. Complete the subtraction sentence.

Sample answers:

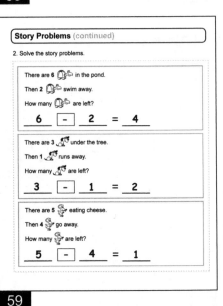

$6 - \underline{3} = 3$

$6 - \underline{2} = 4$

$6 - \underline{5} = 1$

$10 - \underline{9} = 1$

$10 - \underline{3} = 7$

$10 - \underline{6} = 4$

$9 - \underline{5} = 4$

$9 - \underline{3} = 6$

$9 - \underline{7} = 2$

56

Subtraction Facts to 10

1. Draw a line from the subtraction sentences to the correct answer.

$7 - 2 =$ $11 - 1 =$

$8 - 5 =$ $5 - 3 =$

$10 - 0 =$ $9 - 4 =$

$6 - 2 =$ $4 - 2 =$

$8 - 7 =$ $10 - 1 =$

$10 - 2 =$ $8 - 2 =$

$4 - 4 =$ $6 - 3 =$

$10 - 3 =$ $7 - 6 =$

$9 - 5 =$ $1 - 1 =$

1
8
6
2
5
0
10
9
4
3
7

57

Story Problems

1. Solve the story problems.

There are 8 on the ground.
Then 3 go away.
How many are left?

$\underline{8}$ [$-$] $\underline{3}$ $=$ $\underline{5}$

There are 7 on the flower.
Then 4 fly away.
How many are left?

$\underline{7}$ [$-$] $\underline{4}$ $=$ $\underline{3}$

There are 9 on the branch.
Then 3 fly away.
How many are left?

$\underline{9}$ [$-$] $\underline{3}$ $=$ $\underline{6}$

58

Story Problems (continued)

2. Solve the story problems.

There are 6 in the pond.
Then 2 swim away.
How many are left?

$\underline{6}$ [$-$] $\underline{2}$ $=$ $\underline{4}$

There are 3 under the tree.
Then 1 runs away.
How many are left?

$\underline{3}$ [$-$] $\underline{1}$ $=$ $\underline{2}$

There are 5 eating cheese.
Then 4 go away.
How many are left?

$\underline{5}$ [$-$] $\underline{4}$ $=$ $\underline{1}$

59

342

Equal Parts

1. Circle the shape that shows two equal parts. Each part is a half. Colour one half.

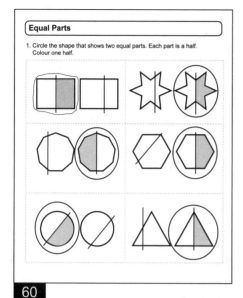

`60`

Naming the Fraction

1. What part is shaded? Circle the fraction.

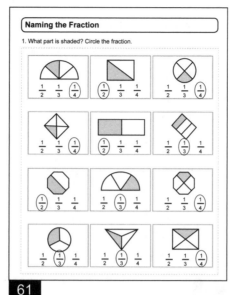

$\frac{1}{2}$ $\frac{1}{3}$ $\frac{1}{4}$

`61`

Colouring One Half

1. Colour one half of the set.

$\frac{1}{2}$ means one part of 2 parts.
One half of the circles are coloured.

Students might colour the halves differently. Sample answers:

Colour $\frac{1}{2}$ green.   Colour $\frac{1}{2}$ red.

Colour $\frac{1}{2}$ blue.   Colour $\frac{1}{2}$ green.

Colour $\frac{1}{2}$ red.   Colour $\frac{1}{2}$ blue.

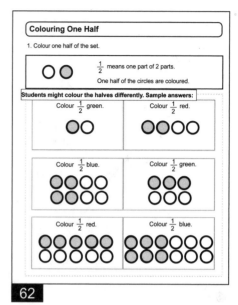

`62`

Repeating Patterns

A **pattern** repeats. A pattern can be different shapes and sizes. The **core** of the pattern are the parts that repeat over and over.

1. Circle the core of each repeating pattern. Extend the pattern.

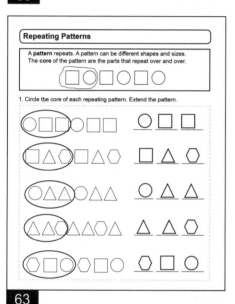

`63`

Repeating Patterns (continued)

2. Circle the core of each repeating pattern. Extend the pattern.

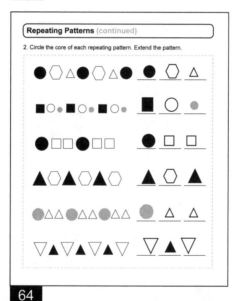

`64`

Using Letters to Name Patterns

1. Use a letter to name each part of the pattern. Circle the core of the pattern.

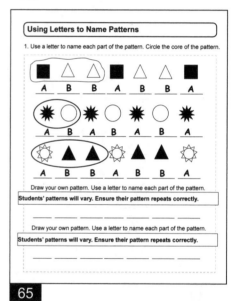

A B B A B B A

A B A B A B A

A B B A B B A

Draw your own pattern. Use a letter to name each part of the pattern.

Students' patterns will vary. Ensure their pattern repeats correctly.

Draw your own pattern. Use a letter to name each part of the pattern.

Students' patterns will vary. Ensure their pattern repeats correctly.

`65`

Creating Patterns

1. Create the pattern. Circle the core.

Colour an AB pattern.

Colour an AAB pattern.

Colour an ABC pattern.

Colour an ABBC pattern.

Make a pattern in which the size of the shape changes.

Students' patterns will vary. Ensure their pattern repeats correctly.

Make a pattern in which the position of the shape changes.

Students' patterns will vary. Ensure their pattern repeats correctly.

`66`

What Comes Next?

1. Make your own patterns. Use two or three colours. Give each pattern a name.

Students' patterns will vary. Ensure their pattern repeats correctly.

Name

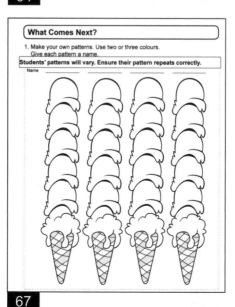

`67`

Getting to Know 2D Shapes

1. Complete.

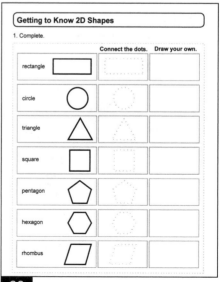

		Connect the dots.	Draw your own.
rectangle			
circle			
triangle			
square			
pentagon			
hexagon			
rhombus			

`68`

Matching 2D Shapes

1. Draw a line from the shape to its name.

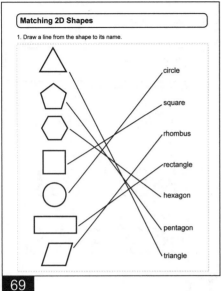

circle

square

rhombus

rectangle

hexagon

pentagon

triangle

What 2D Shapes Do You Know?

1. How many sides and corners does each shape have?

		Number of Sides	Number of Corners
rectangle		4	4
circle		0	0
triangle		3	3
square		4	4
rhombus		4	4
pentagon		5	5

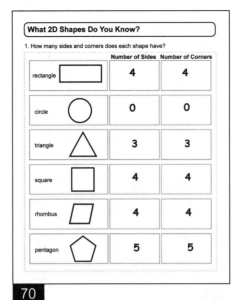

Drawing Shapes

1. Use the shapes to draw a picture.

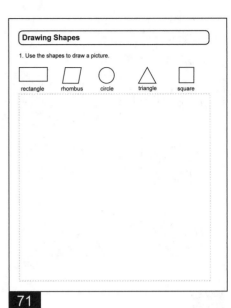

rectangle   rhombus   circle   triangle   square

Sorting 2D Shapes

1. Read the sorting rule. Draw the shapes that follow the rule.

Shapes with **corners**.

Shapes with **less than 4 sides**.

Shapes with **more than 3 sides**.

Shapes with **more than 3 corners**.

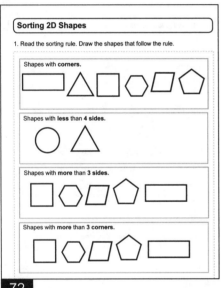

Exploring Symmetry

A line of symmetry divides a object into 2 parts that are the exact same size and shape. Some objects have more than 1 line of symmetry. Some objects do not have a line of symmetry.

line of symmetry

line of symmetry

1. Draw a line of symmetry to show two sides exactly the same.

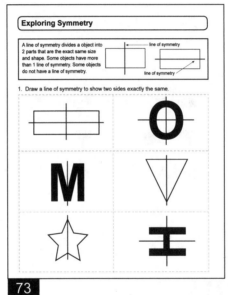

Symmetrical Shapes

1. Draw the other half of each shape.

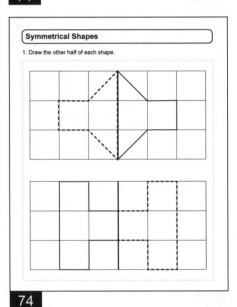

Matching 3D Objects

1. Draw a line from the 3D object to the image it looks like.

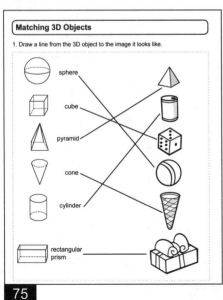

sphere

cube

pyramid

cone

cylinder

rectangular prism

Sorting 3D Objects

1. Read the rule. Circle the objects that follow the rule.

Circle the objects that **can** roll.

Circle the objects that **cannot** roll.

Circle the objects that you **can** stack on each other.

Circle the objects that you **cannot** stack on each other.

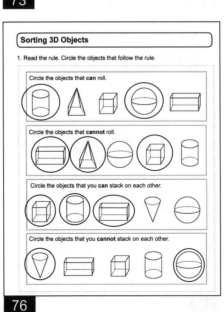

Telling Time to the Hour

A clock has an hour hand.
The hour hand is short. It shows the hour.

You can write the time in two ways. It is **5 o'clock** or **5:00**.

1. Draw a line between the times that are the same.

1 o'clock ———————— 3:00
11:00 ———————— 1:00
3 o'clock ———————— 11 o'clock
5:00 ———————— 5 o'clock

2. Write the time in two ways.

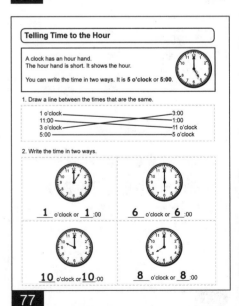

1 o'clock or **1** :00   **6** o'clock or **6** :00

10 o'clock or **10** :00   **8** o'clock or **8** :00

Page 78

2. Tell the time to the hour. Highlight the hour hand blue.
Highlight the minute hand red. Hint: The minute hand is long.

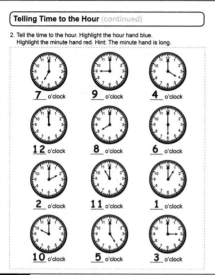

7 o'clock   **9** o'clock   **4** o'clock

12 o'clock   **8** o'clock   **6** o'clock

2 o'clock   **11** o'clock   **1** o'clock

10 o'clock   **5** o'clock   **3** o'clock

78

Page 79

Telling Time to the Half Hour

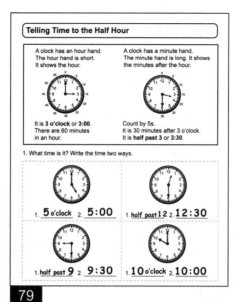

A clock has an hour hand.
The hour hand is short.
It shows the hour.

A clock has a minute hand.
The minute hand is long. It shows
the minutes after the hour.

It is **3 o'clock** or **3:00**.
There are 60 minutes
in an hour.

Count by 5s.
It is 30 minutes after 3 o'clock.
It is **half past 3** or **3:30**.

1. What time is it? Write the time two ways.

1. **5 o'clock** 2. **5:00**   1. **half past 12** 2. **12:30**

1. **half past 9** 2. **9:30**   1. **10 o'clock** 2. **10:00**

79

Page 80

2. Tell the time to the half hour.
Highlight the hour hand blue. Highlight the minute hand red.

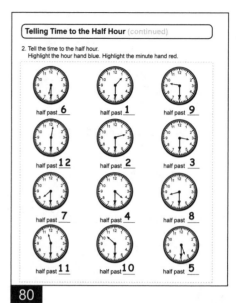

half past **6**   half past **1**   half past **9**

half past **12**   half past **2**   half past **3**

half past **7**   half past **4**   half past **8**

half past **11**   half past **10**   half past **5**

80

Page 81

Showing the Time to the Hour

1. Draw the two hands on the clock to show the time.
Highlight the hour hand blue. Highlight the minute hand red.

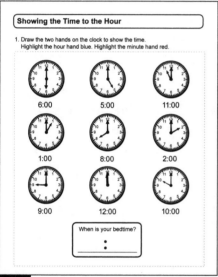

6:00   5:00   11:00

1:00   8:00   2:00

9:00   12:00   10:00

When is your bedtime?

___ : ___

81

Page 82

What Time Is It?

1. Circle the correct time.
Highlight the hour hand blue. Highlight the minute hand red.

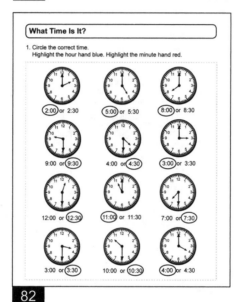

(2:00) or 2:30   (5:00) or 5:30   (8:00) or 8:30

9:00 or (9:30)   4:00 or (4:30)   (3:00) or 3:30

12:00 or (12:30)   (11:00) or 11:30   7:00 or (7:30)

3:00 or (3:30)   10:00 or (10:30)   (4:00) or 4:30

82

Page 83

Canadian Coins

Each Canadian coin has a value.

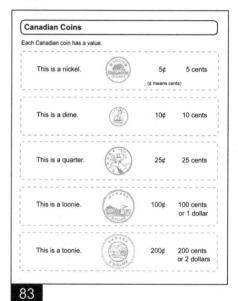

This is a nickel.		5¢	5 cents
		(¢ means cents)	
This is a dime.		10¢	10 cents
This is a quarter.		25¢	25 cents
This is a loonie.		100¢	100 cents or 1 dollar
This is a toonie.		200¢	200 cents or 2 dollars

83

Page 84

Getting to Know Coins

1. Draw a line from the coin to its value.
Then draw a line from the coin to its name.

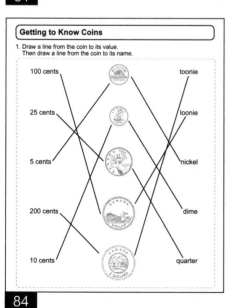

100 cents   toonie

25 cents   loonie

5 cents   nickel

200 cents   dime

10 cents   quarter

84

Page 85

2. Circle the loonies red.   Circle the quarters green.
Circle the dimes blue.   Circle the nickels yellow.
Circle the toonies orange.

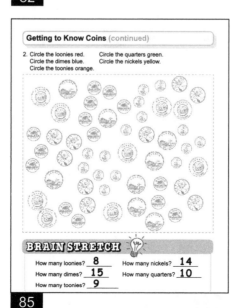

BRAIN STRETCH

How many loonies? **8**   How many nickels? **14**

How many dimes? **15**   How many quarters? **10**

How many toonies? **9**

85

Page 86

Counting Nickels

1. Count by 5s to find the value of the nickels.

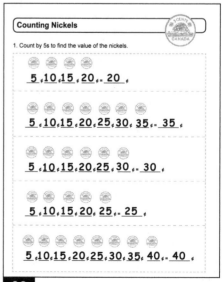

5, **10**, **15**, **20**, = **20** ¢

5, **10**, **15**, **20**, **25**, **30**, **35**, = **35** ¢

5, **10**, **15**, **20**, **25**, **30**, = **30** ¢

5, **10**, **15**, **20**, **25**, = **25** ¢

5, **10**, **15**, **20**, **25**, **30**, **35**, **40**, = **40** ¢

86

Counting Dimes

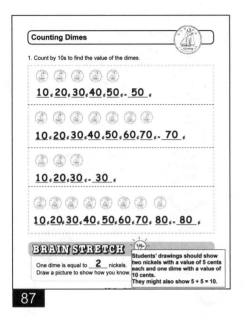

1. Count by 10s to find the value of the dimes.

10, 20, 30, 40, 50, **50** ¢

10, 20, 30, 40, 50, 60, 70, **70** ¢

10, 20, 30, **30** ¢

10, 20, 30, 40, 50, 60, 70, 80, **80** ¢

BRAIN STRETCH

One dime is equal to **2** nickels.
Draw a picture to show how you know.

Students' drawings should show two nickels with a value of 5 cents each and one dime with a value of 10 cents.
They might also show 5 + 5 = 10.

87

Toy Counter

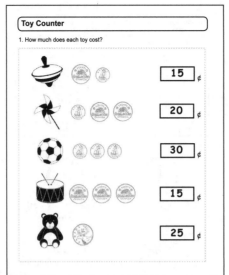

1. How much does each toy cost?

15	¢
20	¢
30	¢
15	¢
25	¢

88

Exploring Pictographs

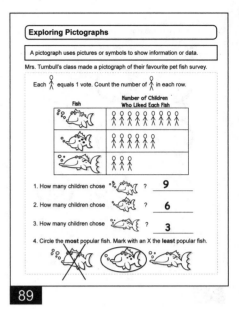

A pictograph uses pictures or symbols to show information or data.

Mrs. Turnbull's class made a pictograph of their favourite pet fish survey.

Each ⅄ equals 1 vote. Count the number of ⅄ in each row.

1. How many children chose 🐟 ? **9**

2. How many children chose 🐟 ? **6**

3. How many children chose 🐟 ? **3**

4. Circle the **most** popular fish. Mark with an X the **least** popular fish.

89

Exploring Bar Graphs

A bar graph uses bars to show data.
This bar graph shows the favourite winter activity of children.

Read the bar graph to answer the questions.

Favourite Winter Activity

1. How many votes? **6**   **4**   **7**

2. Circle the **most** popular winter activity.

3. Circle the **least** popular winter activity.

90

Exploring Bar Graphs (continued)

Ms. Stanley's class took a survey of their favourite pets.
Count the votes for each pet and complete the bar graph.

Favourite Pet Survey

1. How many votes? **7**   **3**   **5**

2. Circle the pet that 3 children chose as their favourite pet.

91

Exploring Tally Charts

A tally chart counts data in 1s and groups of 5.

Each single tally mark stands for 1 vote. | Each group of five tally marks stands for 5 votes. ||||

Ms. Yen's class made a tally chart of their favourite ice cream.
Count the tally marks.

Favourite Ice Cream Flavour

Flavour	Tally	Total
vanilla	‖‖‖ ‖‖‖ ‖‖‖	15
chocolate	‖‖‖ ||||	9
strawberry	|||	3

1. How many children picked vanilla? **15**

2. How many children picked chocolate? **9**

3. How many children picked strawberry? **3**

4. Which ice cream was **most** popular? **vanilla**

5. Which ice cream was **least** popular? **stawberry**

92

Shortest to Tallest

1. Number the creatures in order from shortest to tallest. Use 1, 2, and 3.

1	3	2
3	1	2
2	1	3
1	3	2

93

Tallest to Shortest

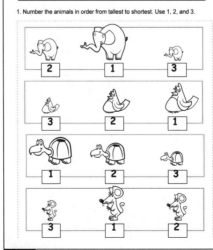

1. Number the animals in order from tallest to shortest. Use 1, 2, and 3.

2	1	3
3	2	1
1	2	3
3	1	2

94

Exploring Measuring

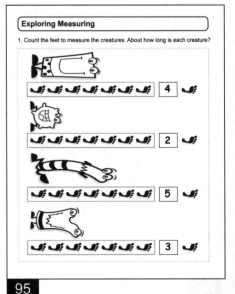

1. Count the feet to measure the creatures. About how long is each creature?

4	🐾
2	🐾
5	🐾
3	🐾

95

Exploring Measuring (continued)

2. Count the stars to measure the pencils.
About how long is each pencil?

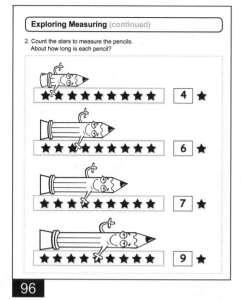

4 ★

6 ★

7 ★

9 ★

Exploring Measuring (continued)

3. How many centimetres long is each pencil?

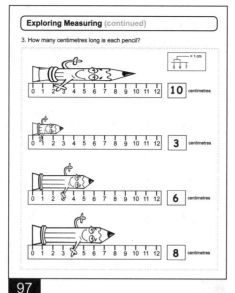

= 1 cm

10 centimetres

3 centimetres

6 centimetres

8 centimetres

Exploring Measuring (continued)

4. Find an object and then measure in centimetres.

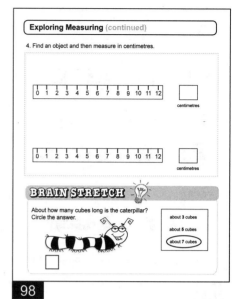

centimetres

centimetres

BRAIN STRETCH

About how many cubes long is the caterpillar?
Circle the answer.

about 3 cubes
about 5 cubes
about 7 cubes

Exploring Mass

Mass measures how much something weighs.

1. What is the mass of the creature? Count the blocks to find out.

8 blocks

11 blocks

13 blocks

8 blocks

Exploring Mass (continued)

2. Some blocks are missing. Draw blocks to make the same mass on both sides.

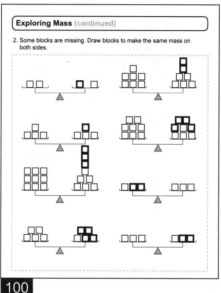

Addition Doubles

1. Write the number sentence.

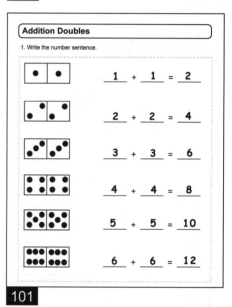

1 + 1 = 2

2 + 2 = 4

3 + 3 = 6

4 + 4 = 8

5 + 5 = 10

6 + 6 = 12

Addition Doubles Plus 1

1. Use doubles plus 1 to add.

If 6 + 6 = 12   If 1 + 1 = 2
Then 6 + 7 = 13   Then 1 + 2 = 3

If 9 + 9 = 18   If 5 + 5 = 10
Then 9 + 10 = 19   Then 5 + 6 = 11

If 8 + 8 = 16   If 10 + 10 = 20
Then 8 + 9 = 17   Then 10 + 11 = 21

If 3 + 3 = 6   If 2 + 2 = 4
Then 3 + 4 = 7   Then 2 + 3 = 5

If 7 + 7 = 14   If 4 + 4 = 8
Then 7 + 8 = 15   Then 4 + 5 = 9

Adding by Making 10

1. Make a group of 10 to help you add.

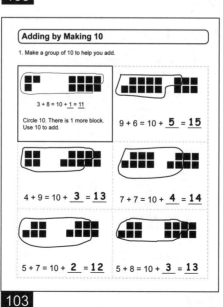

3 + 8 = 10 + 1 = 11

Circle 10. There is 1 more block.
Use 10 to add.

9 + 6 = 10 + 5 = 15

4 + 9 = 10 + 3 = 13

7 + 7 = 10 + 4 = 14

5 + 7 = 10 + 2 = 12

5 + 8 = 10 + 3 = 13

Adding by Making 10 (continued)

2. Make a group of 10 to help you add.

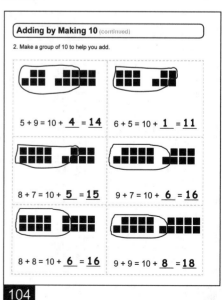

5 + 9 = 10 + 4 = 14

6 + 5 = 10 + 1 = 11

8 + 7 = 10 + 5 = 15

9 + 7 = 10 + 6 = 16

8 + 8 = 10 + 6 = 16

9 + 9 = 10 + 8 = 18

96

97

98

99

100

101

102

103

104

Panel 105

Adding by Making 10 (continued)

3. Make a group of 10 to help you add.

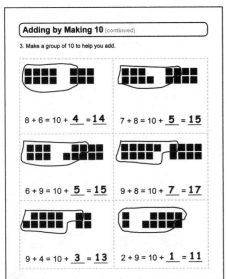

$8 + 6 = 10 + \underline{4} = \underline{14}$

$7 + 8 = 10 + \underline{5} = \underline{15}$

$6 + 9 = 10 + \underline{5} = \underline{15}$

$9 + 8 = 10 + \underline{7} = \underline{17}$

$9 + 4 = 10 + \underline{3} = \underline{13}$

$2 + 9 = 10 + \underline{1} = \underline{11}$

`105`

Panel 106

Addition Practice—Sums from 11 to 15

1. Add. Use the number line or counters to help you add.
Hint: Start with the greater number.

0 1 2 3 4 5 6 7 8 9 10 11 12 13 14 15 16 17 18 19 20

8	9	10	9	14
+ 6	+ 3	+ 5	+ 6	+ 3
14	**12**	**15**	**15**	**17**

5	10	11	8	7
+ 6	+ 5	+ 3	+ 4	+ 7
11	**15**	**14**	**12**	**14**

10	6	13	9	7
+ 3	+ 6	+ 1	+ 4	+ 6
13	**12**	**14**	**13**	**13**

9	5	9	8	10
+ 5	+ 7	+ 2	+ 5	+ 2
14	**12**	**11**	**13**	**12**

`106`

Panel 107

Addition Practice—Sums from 16 to 20

1. Use the number line or counters to help you add.

0 1 2 3 4 5 6 7 8 9 10 11 12 13 14 15 16 17 18 19 20

9	6	16	8	10
+ 8	+ 10	+ 2	+ 8	+ 7
17	**16**	**18**	**16**	**17**

17	16	14	12	14
+ 2	+ 0	+ 6	+ 5	+ 2
19	**16**	**20**	**17**	**16**

8	12	9	18	9
+ 10	+ 4	+ 10	+ 2	+ 9
18	**16**	**19**	**20**	**18**

11	11	7	15	10
+ 6	+ 8	+ 9	+ 3	+ 10
17	**19**	**16**	**18**	**20**

`107`

Panel 108

Math Riddle: Addition Facts to 20

What kind of socks do bears wear?

Watch out! Some letters are not used in the riddle!

T	H	E	Y		P	R	E	F	E	R
13	10	16	8		20	11	16	9	16	11

T	H	E	I	R		B	E	A	R		F	E	E	T!
13	10	16	17	11		6	16	13	11		9	16	16	13

A	B	C	E
$6 + 7 = \underline{13}$	$2 + 4 = \underline{6}$	$7 + 5 = \underline{12}$	$8 + 8 = \underline{16}$

F	H	I	L
$4 + 5 = \underline{9}$	$5 + 5 = \underline{10}$	$10 + 7 = \underline{17}$	$8 + 7 = \underline{15}$

M	P	Q	R
$3 + 4 = \underline{7}$	$19 + 1 = \underline{20}$	$9 + 9 = \underline{18}$	$5 + 6 = \underline{11}$

S	T	W	Y
$7 + 7 = \underline{14}$	$6 + 7 = \underline{13}$	$1 + 4 = \underline{5}$	$3 + 5 = \underline{8}$

`108`

Panel 109

Using a Number Line to Subtract

Subtract using a number line.

$12 - 3 = \underline{9}$

0 1 2 3 4 5 6 7 8 9 10 11 12 13 14 15 16 17 18 19 20

SAY: 11, 10, 9

Mark a dot at 12.
Draw 3 steps to count back.
Stop at 9.

1. Use the number line to subtract. Mark a dot to show where you start.
Then count back by drawing the steps. Write the answer.

$15 - 1 = \underline{14}$ 0 1 2 3 4 5 6 7 8 9 10 11 12 13 14 15 16 17 18 19 20

$19 - 4 = \underline{15}$ 0 1 2 3 4 5 6 7 8 9 10 11 12 13 14 15 16 17 18 19 20

$13 - 3 = \underline{10}$ 0 1 2 3 4 5 6 7 8 9 10 11 12 13 14 15 16 17 18 19 20

$17 - 6 = \underline{11}$ 0 1 2 3 4 5 6 7 8 9 10 11 12 13 14 15 16 17 18 19 20

`109`

Panel 110

Subtraction Match

1. Draw a line from the number sentence to the correct answer.

12 – 3	1	11 – 3
16 – 8	2	18 – 9
10 – 5	3	9 – 8
6 – 3	4	12 – 9
17 – 10	5	13 – 6
20 – 10	6	7 – 5
8 – 4	7	14 – 7
11 – 9	8	8 – 3
13 – 7	9	10 – 0
5 – 4	10	13 – 9

`110`

Panel 111

Subtracting 1 or 2 by Counting Back

1. Count back to subtract.

$14 - 1 = \underline{13}$ 14, **13**	$19 - 2 = \underline{17}$ 19, **18**, **17**
$17 - 1 = \underline{16}$ 17, **16**	$18 - 2 = \underline{16}$ 18, **17**, **16**
$16 - 1 = \underline{15}$ 16, **15**	$20 - 2 = \underline{18}$ 20, **19**, **18**
$15 - 1 = \underline{14}$ 15, **14**	$14 - 2 = \underline{12}$ 14, **13**, **12**
$19 - 1 = \underline{18}$ 19, **18**	$13 - 2 = \underline{11}$ 13, **12**, **11**
$13 - 1 = \underline{12}$ 13, **12**	$16 - 2 = \underline{14}$ 16, **15**, **14**
$20 - 1 = \underline{19}$ 20, **19**	$15 - 2 = \underline{13}$ 15, **14**, **13**

`111`

Panel 112

Making 10 to Subtract

1. Make 10 to make an easier problem. Then subtract.

$12 - 9 =$
$12 - 9 = \underline{13} - 10 = \underline{3}$
I know 9 + 1 = 10.
So, I add 1 to each number.
Then I subtract to get the answer.

$19 - 6 =$
$19 - 6 = \underline{23} - 10 = \underline{13}$
Add 4 to each number.

$15 - 7 =$
$15 - 7 = \underline{18} - 10 = \underline{8}$
Add **3** to each number.

$14 - 8 =$
$14 - 8 = \underline{16} - 10 = \underline{6}$
Add **2** to each number.

$18 - 7 =$
$18 - 7 = \underline{21} - 10 = \underline{11}$
Add **3** to each number.

$13 - 9 =$
$13 - 9 = \underline{14} - 10 = \underline{4}$
Add **1** to each number.

$17 - 6 =$
$17 - 6 = \underline{21} - 10 = \underline{11}$
Add **4** to each number.

$16 - 7 =$
$16 - 7 = \underline{19} - 10 = \underline{9}$
Add **3** to each number.

`112`

Panel 113

Subtracting by 7, 8, or 9 from 11 to 20

1. Find each difference. You can subtract by counting back or use counters to help.

14	11	14	16	10
– 9	– 7	– 8	– 9	– 9
5	**4**	**6**	**7**	**1**

15	12	18	13	16
– 8	– 7	– 8	– 9	– 7
7	**5**	**10**	**4**	**9**

12	19	16	14	11
– 9	– 9	– 8	– 7	– 9
3	**10**	**8**	**7**	**2**

15	13	17	19	20
– 7	– 8	– 9	– 8	– 8
8	**5**	**8**	**11**	**12**

17	11	15	20	12
– 7	– 8	– 9	– 7	– 8
10	**3**	**6**	**13**	**4**

`113`

Page 114

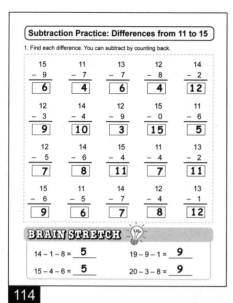

Subtraction Practice: Differences from 11 to 15

1. Find each difference. You can subtract by counting back.

15 − 9 = **6**	11 − 7 = **4**	13 − 7 = **6**	12 − 8 = **4**	14 − 2 = **12**
12 − 3 = **9**	14 − 4 = **10**	12 − 9 = **3**	15 − 0 = **15**	11 − 6 = **5**
12 − 5 = **7**	14 − 6 = **8**	15 − 4 = **11**	11 − 4 = **7**	13 − 2 = **11**
15 − 6 = **9**	11 − 5 = **6**	14 − 7 = **7**	12 − 4 = **8**	13 − 1 = **12**

BRAIN STRETCH

14 − 1 − 8 = **5**   19 − 9 − 1 = **9**

15 − 4 − 6 = **5**   20 − 3 − 8 = **9**

114

Page 115

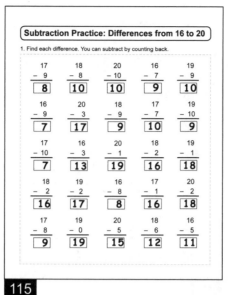

Subtraction Practice: Differences from 16 to 20

1. Find each difference. You can subtract by counting back.

17 − 9 = **8**	18 − 8 = **10**	20 − 10 = **10**	16 − 7 = **9**	19 − 9 = **10**
16 − 9 = **7**	20 − 3 = **17**	18 − 9 = **9**	17 − 7 = **10**	19 − 10 = **9**
17 − 10 = **7**	16 − 3 = **13**	20 − 1 = **19**	18 − 2 = **16**	19 − 1 = **18**
18 − 2 = **16**	19 − 2 = **17**	16 − 8 = **8**	17 − 1 = **16**	20 − 2 = **18**
17 − 8 = **9**	19 − 0 = **19**	20 − 5 = **15**	18 − 6 = **12**	16 − 5 = **11**

115

Page 116

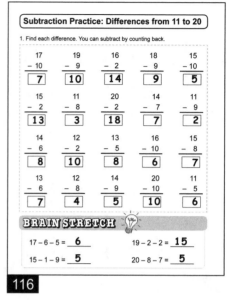

Subtraction Practice: Differences from 11 to 20

1. Find each difference. You can subtract by counting back.

17 − 10 = **7**	19 − 9 = **10**	16 − 2 = **14**	18 − 9 = **9**	15 − 10 = **5**
15 − 2 = **13**	11 − 8 = **3**	20 − 2 = **18**	14 − 7 = **7**	11 − 9 = **2**
14 − 6 = **8**	12 − 2 = **10**	13 − 5 = **8**	16 − 10 = **6**	15 − 8 = **7**
13 − 6 = **7**	12 − 8 = **4**	14 − 9 = **5**	20 − 10 = **10**	11 − 5 = **6**

BRAIN STRETCH

17 − 6 − 5 = **6**   19 − 2 − 2 = **15**

15 − 1 − 9 = **5**   20 − 8 − 7 = **5**

116

Page 117

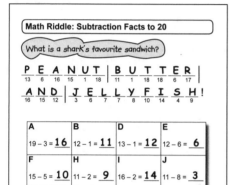

Math Riddle: Subtraction Facts to 20

What is a shark's favourite sandwich?

P E A N U T | B U T T E R |
13 6 16 15 1 18 | 11 1 18 18 6 17

A N D | J E L L Y F I S H !
16 15 12 | 3 6 7 7 8 10 14 4 9

A	B	D	E
19 − 3 = **16**	12 − 1 = **11**	13 − 1 = **12**	12 − 6 = **6**
F	**H**	**I**	**J**
15 − 5 = **10**	11 − 2 = **9**	16 − 2 = **14**	11 − 8 = **3**
L	**N**	**P**	**R**
9 − 2 = **7**	17 − 2 = **15**	16 − 3 = **13**	17 − 0 = **17**
S	**T**	**U**	**Y**
8 − 4 = **4**	20 − 2 = **18**	10 − 9 = **1**	10 − 2 = **8**

117

Page 118

How to Use the Addition Table

The numbers in the dark border down the side show the rows. The numbers in the dark border at the top show the columns. You can use this table to add to find the sum of two numbers.
For example, find the sum of 6 + 5.

First way: Go down to the 6 row. Put your finger on the 6. Then slide your finger along the 6 row to the 5 column. The number in the square is your answer! So, 6 + 5 = 11.

Second way: Go down to the 5 row. Then slide your finger along the 5 row to the 6 column to get your answer.

Third way: Go to the 6 column. Then slide your finger down to the 5 row to get your answer.

+	0	1	2	3	4	5	6	7	8	9	10
0	0	1	2	3	4	5	6	7	8	9	10
1	1	2	3	4	5	6	7	8	9	10	11
2	2	3	4	5	6	7	8	9	10	11	12
3	3	4	5	6	7	8	9	10	11	12	13
4	4	5	6	7	8	9	10	11	12	13	14
5	5	6	7	8	9	10	11	12	13	14	15
6	6	7	8	9	10	11	12	13	14	15	16
7	7	8	9	10	11	12	13	14	15	16	17
8	8	9	10	11	12	13	14	15	16	17	18
9	9	10	11	12	13	14	15	16	17	18	19
10	10	11	12	13	14	15	16	17	18	19	20

118

Page 119

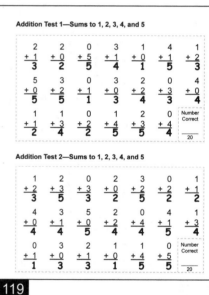

Addition Test 1—Sums to 1, 2, 3, 4, and 5

2 + 1 = 3	2 + 0 = 2	0 + 5 = 5	3 + 1 = 4	1 + 0 = 1	4 + 1 = 5	1 + 2 = 3
5 + 0 = 5	3 + 2 = 5	0 + 1 = 1	3 + 0 = 3	2 + 2 = 4	0 + 3 = 3	4 + 0 = 4
1 + 1 = 2	1 + 3 = 4	0 + 2 = 2	1 + 4 = 5	2 + 3 = 5	0 + 4 = 4	Number Correct __/20

Addition Test 2—Sums to 1, 2, 3, 4, and 5

1 + 2 = 3	2 + 3 = 5	0 + 3 = 3	2 + 0 = 2	3 + 2 = 5	0 + 2 = 2	1 + 1 = 2
4 + 0 = 4	3 + 1 = 4	5 + 0 = 5	2 + 2 = 4	0 + 4 = 4	4 + 1 = 5	1 + 3 = 4
0 + 1 = 1	3 + 0 = 3	2 + 1 = 3	1 + 0 = 1	1 + 4 = 5	0 + 5 = 5	Number Correct __/20

119

Page 120

Addition Test 3—Sums to 1, 2, 3, 4, and 5

2 + 2 = 4	3 + 0 = 3	0 + 5 = 5	3 + 2 = 5	1 + 0 = 1	4 + 1 = 5	1 + 2 = 3
5 + 0 = 5	0 + 2 = 2	1 + 3 = 4	2 + 1 = 3	1 + 4 = 5	0 + 3 = 3	4 + 0 = 4
1 + 1 = 2	3 + 1 = 4	2 + 0 = 2	2 + 3 = 5	0 + 1 = 1	0 + 4 = 4	Number Correct __/20

Addition Test 4—Sums to 1, 2, 3, 4, and 5

1 + 2 = 3	2 + 3 = 5	0 + 3 = 3	2 + 0 = 2	3 + 2 = 5	0 + 2 = 2	1 + 1 = 2
0 + 5 = 5	1 + 0 = 1	2 + 2 = 4	5 + 0 = 5	0 + 4 = 4	4 + 0 = 4	1 + 3 = 4
0 + 1 = 1	2 + 1 = 3	3 + 0 = 3	1 + 4 = 5	0 + 4 = 4	4 + 1 = 5	Number Correct __/20

120

Page 121

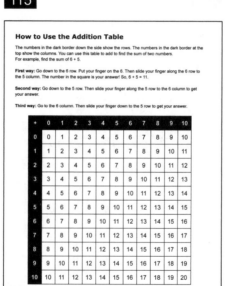

Addition Test 5—Sums to 1, 2, 3, 4, and 5

3 + 0 = 3	5 + 0 = 5	4 + 1 = 5	0 + 5 = 5	1 + 0 = 1	2 + 3 = 5	0 + 1 = 1
0 + 4 = 4	3 + 2 = 5	0 + 3 = 3	1 + 2 = 3	2 + 1 = 3	4 + 0 = 4	3 + 1 = 4
2 + 2 = 4	1 + 4 = 5	0 + 2 = 2	1 + 3 = 4	2 + 0 = 2	1 + 1 = 2	Number Correct __/20

Addition Test 6—Sums to 1, 2, 3, 4, and 5

3 + 2 = 5	1 + 3 = 4	0 + 3 = 3	5 + 0 = 5	2 + 2 = 4	0 + 2 = 2	4 + 1 = 5
3 + 1 = 4	0 + 1 = 1	2 + 1 = 3	1 + 4 = 5	1 + 0 = 1	4 + 0 = 4	1 + 3 = 4
0 + 1 = 1	2 + 1 = 3	3 + 0 = 3	2 + 0 = 2	0 + 4 = 4	0 + 5 = 5	Number Correct __/20

121

Page 122

Addition Test 7—Sums to 1, 2, 3, 4, and 5

1 + 1 = 2	5 + 0 = 5	2 + 3 = 5	2 + 2 = 4	0 + 2 = 2	2 + 1 = 3	4 + 0 = 4
2 + 0 = 2	3 + 2 = 5	0 + 4 = 4	0 + 5 = 5	1 + 0 = 1	3 + 1 = 4	4 + 1 = 5
1 + 2 = 3	0 + 1 = 1	1 + 3 = 4	1 + 4 = 5	0 + 3 = 3	3 + 0 = 3	Number Correct __/20

Addition Test 8—Sums to 1, 2, 3, 4, and 5

1 + 2 = 3	2 + 3 = 5	1 + 1 = 2	2 + 0 = 2	3 + 2 = 5	0 + 2 = 2	3 + 0 = 3
0 + 4 = 4	1 + 2 = 3	2 + 2 = 4	5 + 0 = 5	0 + 3 = 3	4 + 1 = 5	1 + 3 = 4
0 + 1 = 1	5 + 0 = 5	3 + 1 = 4	1 + 0 = 1	0 + 4 = 4	4 + 0 = 4	Number Correct __/20

122

Addition Test 9—Sums to 1, 2, 3, 4, and 5

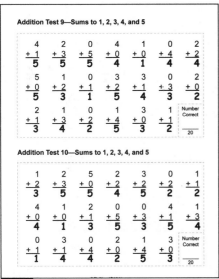

4+1=5 2+3=5 0+5=5 4+0=4 1+0=1 0+4=4 2+2=4
5+0=5 1+2=3 0+1=1 3+2=5 3+1=4 0+3=3 2+0=2
2+1=3 1+3=4 0+2=2 1+4=5 3+0=3 1+1=2   Number Correct /20

Addition Test 10—Sums to 1, 2, 3, 4, and 5

1+2=3 2+3=5 5+0=5 2+2=4 3+2=5 0+2=2 1+1=2
4+0=4 1+0=1 2+1=3 0+5=5 0+3=3 4+1=5 1+3=4
0+1=1 3+1=4 0+4=4 1+1=2 2+3=5 3+0=3   Number Correct /20

Addition Test 1—Sums to 6, 7, 8, 9, and 10

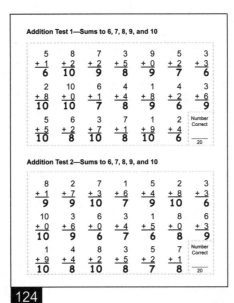

5+1=6 8+2=10 7+2=9 3+5=8 9+0=9 5+2=7 3+3=6
2+8=10 10+0=10 6+1=7 4+4=8 1+8=9 4+2=6 3+6=9
5+5=10 6+2=8 3+7=10 7+1=8 1+9=10 2+4=6   Number Correct /20

Addition Test 2—Sums to 6, 7, 8, 9, and 10

8+1=9 2+7=9 7+3=10 1+6=7 5+4=9 2+8=10 3+3=6
10+0=10 3+6=9 6+0=6 3+4=7 1+5=6 8+0=8 6+3=9
1+9=10 4+4=8 8+2=10 3+5=8 5+2=7 5+3=8   Number Correct /20

Addition Test 3—Sums to 6, 7, 8, 9, and 10

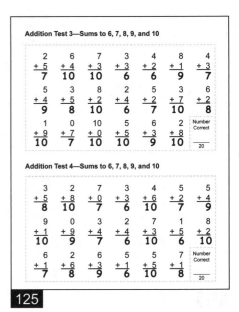

2+5=7 6+4=10 7+3=10 3+3=6 4+2=6 8+1=9 4+3=7
5+4=9 3+5=8 8+2=10 2+4=6 5+2=7 3+7=10 6+2=8
1+9=10 0+7=7 10+0=10 5+5=10 6+3=9 2+8=10   Number Correct /20

Addition Test 4—Sums to 6, 7, 8, 9, and 10

3+5=8 2+8=10 7+0=7 3+3=6 4+6=10 5+2=7 5+4=9
9+1=10 0+9=9 3+4=7 2+4=6 7+3=10 1+5=6 8+2=10
6+1=7 2+6=8 6+3=9 5+1=6 5+5=10 7+1=8   Number Correct /20

Addition Test 5—Sums to 6, 7, 8, 9, and 10

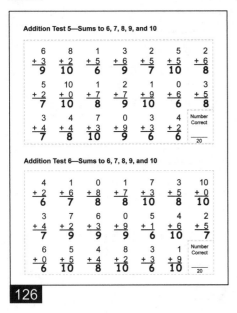

6+3=9 8+2=10 1+5=6 3+6=9 2+5=7 5+5=10 2+6=8
5+2=7 10+0=10 1+7=8 2+7=9 1+9=10 0+6=6 3+5=8
3+4=7 4+4=8 7+3=10 0+9=9 3+3=6 4+2=6   Number Correct /20

Addition Test 6—Sums to 6, 7, 8, 9, and 10

4+2=6 1+6=7 0+8=8 1+7=8 7+3=10 3+5=8 10+0=10
3+4=7 7+2=9 6+3=9 0+9=9 5+1=6 4+6=10 2+5=7
6+0=6 5+5=10 4+4=8 8+2=10 3+3=6 1+9=10   Number Correct /20

Addition Test 7—Sums to 6, 7, 8, 9, and 10

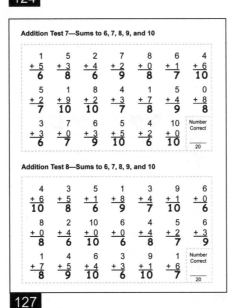

1+5=6 5+3=8 2+4=6 7+2=9 8+0=8 6+1=7 4+6=10
5+2=7 1+9=10 8+2=10 4+3=7 1+7=8 5+4=9 0+8=8
3+3=6 7+3=10 6+3=9 5+5=10 4+2=6 10+0=10   Number Correct /20

Addition Test 8—Sums to 6, 7, 8, 9, and 10

4+6=10 3+5=8 5+1=6 1+8=9 3+4=7 9+1=10 6+0=6
8+0=8 2+4=6 10+0=10 6+0=6 4+4=8 5+2=7 6+3=9
1+7=8 4+5=9 6+4=10 3+3=6 9+1=10 1+6=7   Number Correct /20

Addition Test 9—Sums to 6, 7, 8, 9, and 10

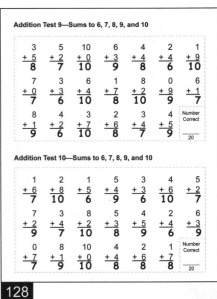

3+5=8 5+2=7 10+0=10 6+3=9 4+4=8 2+4=6 1+9=10
7+0=7 3+3=6 6+4=10 1+7=8 8+2=10 0+9=9 6+1=7
8+1=9 4+2=6 3+7=10 2+6=8 3+4=7 4+5=9   Number Correct /20

Addition Test 10—Sums to 6, 7, 8, 9, and 10

1+6=7 2+8=10 1+5=6 5+4=9 3+3=6 4+6=10 5+2=7
7+2=9 3+4=7 8+2=10 5+3=8 4+5=9 2+4=6 6+3=9
0+7=7 8+1=9 10+0=10 4+4=8 2+6=8 1+7=8   Number Correct /20

Addition Test 1—Sums to 11, 12, 13, 14, and 15

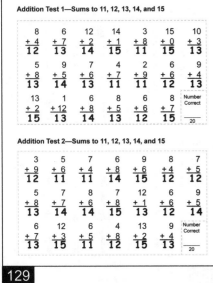

8+4=12 6+7=13 12+2=14 14+1=15 3+8=11 15+0=15 10+3=13
5+8=13 9+5=14 7+6=13 4+7=11 2+9=11 6+6=12 9+4=13
13+2=15 1+12=13 6+8=14 8+5=13 6+6=12 8+7=15   Number Correct /20

Addition Test 2—Sums to 11, 12, 13, 14, and 15

3+9=12 5+6=11 7+4=11 6+8=14 9+6=15 8+4=12 7+5=12
5+8=13 7+7=14 8+6=14 7+8=15 12+1=13 6+6=12 9+5=14
6+7=13 12+3=15 6+5=11 4+8=12 13+2=15 9+4=13   Number Correct /20

Addition Test 3—Sums to 11, 12, 13, 14, and 15

6+9=15 11+2=13 9+3=12 13+1=14 8+4=12 7+6=13 9+4=13
12+0=12 14+1=15 8+5=13 7+7=14 1+13=14 10+3=13 10+5=15
6+5=11 8+6=14 7+8=15 3+8=11 12+1=13 5+9=14   Number Correct /20

Addition Test 4—Sums to 11, 12, 13, 14, and 15

5+8=13 4+9=13 10+5=15 8+7=15 10+2=12 6+8=14 5+6=11
9+2=11 6+6=12 7+4=11 11+3=14 5+9=14 12+2=14 3+8=11
4+7=11 13+2=15 6+5=11 13+1=14 3+9=12 9+6=15   Number Correct /20

Addition Test 5—Sums to 11, 12, 13, 14, and 15

8+4=12 6+5=11 12+3=15 4+9=13 5+7=12 10+5=15 7+7=14
7+8=15 7+4=11 9+6=15 6+6=12 10+3=13 12+2=14 14+1=15
6+8=14 8+5=13 7+6=13 6+9=15 5+8=13 4+7=11   Number Correct /20

Addition Test 6—Sums to 11, 12, 13, 14, and 15

3+9=12 6+6=12 7+7=14 8+7=15 10+3=13 13+1=14 6+5=11
1+14=15 7+5=12 8+3=11 5+6=11 9+4=13 6+8=14 10+5=15
4+8=12 3+10=13 4+7=11 7+6=13 12+3=15 9+5=14   Number Correct /20

Addition Test 7—Sums to 11, 12, 13, 14, and 15

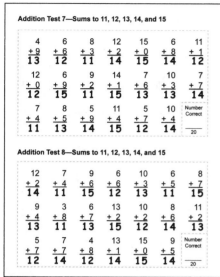

4 +9 = 13	6 +6 = 12	8 +3 = 11	12 +2 = 14	15 +0 = 15	6 +8 = 14	11 +1 = 12
12 +0 = 12	6 +9 = 15	9 +2 = 11	14 +1 = 15	7 +6 = 13	10 +3 = 13	7 +7 = 14
7 +4 = 11	8 +5 = 13	5 +9 = 14	11 +4 = 15	5 +7 = 12	10 +4 = 14	Number Correct /20

Addition Test 8—Sums to 11, 12, 13, 14, and 15

12 +2 = 14	7 +4 = 11	9 +6 = 15	6 +6 = 12	10 +3 = 13	6 +5 = 11	8 +7 = 15
9 +4 = 13	3 +8 = 11	6 +7 = 13	13 +2 = 15	10 +2 = 12	8 +6 = 14	11 +2 = 13
5 +7 = 12	7 +7 = 14	4 +8 = 12	13 +1 = 14	15 +0 = 15	9 +5 = 14	Number Correct /20

132

Addition Test 9—Sums to 11, 12, 13, 14, and 15

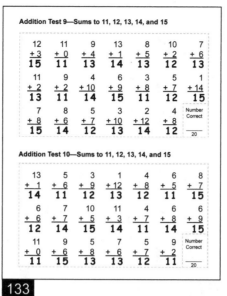

12 +3 = 15	11 +0 = 11	9 +4 = 13	13 +1 = 14	8 +5 = 13	10 +2 = 12	7 +6 = 13
11 +2 = 13	9 +2 = 11	4 +10 = 14	6 +9 = 15	3 +8 = 11	5 +7 = 12	1 +14 = 15
7 +8 = 15	8 +6 = 14	5 +7 = 12	3 +10 = 13	2 +12 = 14	4 +8 = 12	Number Correct /20

Addition Test 10—Sums to 11, 12, 13, 14, and 15

13 +1 = 14	5 +6 = 11	3 +9 = 12	1 +12 = 13	4 +8 = 12	6 +5 = 11	8 +7 = 15
6 +6 = 12	7 +7 = 14	10 +5 = 15	11 +3 = 14	4 +7 = 11	6 +8 = 14	6 +9 = 15
11 +0 = 11	9 +6 = 15	5 +8 = 13	7 +6 = 13	5 +7 = 12	9 +2 = 11	Number Correct /20

133

Addition Test 1—Sums to 16, 17, 18, 19, and 20

16 +3 = 19	7 +9 = 16	9 +10 = 19	13 +4 = 17	15 +2 = 17	18 +2 = 20	9 +7 = 16
19 +1 = 20	8 +9 = 17	20 +0 = 20	17 +0 = 17	10 +10 = 20	10 +8 = 18	17 +1 = 18
16 +2 = 18	8 +8 = 16	15 +3 = 18	14 +2 = 16	10 +7 = 17	9 +9 = 18	Number Correct /20

Addition Test 2—Sums to 16, 17, 18, 19, and 20

13 +4 = 17	19 +1 = 20	7 +9 = 16	15 +1 = 16	15 +4 = 19	16 +1 = 17	3 +17 = 20
19 +1 = 20	10 +8 = 18	16 +3 = 19	13 +3 = 16	5 +12 = 17	8 +8 = 16	10 +7 = 17
20 +0 = 20	15 +2 = 17	9 +9 = 18	7 +10 = 17	10 +10 = 20	9 +8 = 17	Number Correct /20

134

Addition Test 3—Sums to 16, 17, 18, 19, and 20

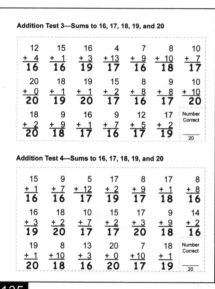

12 +4 = 16	15 +1 = 16	16 +3 = 19	4 +13 = 17	7 +9 = 16	8 +10 = 18	10 +7 = 17
20 +0 = 20	18 +1 = 19	19 +1 = 20	15 +2 = 17	8 +8 = 16	9 +8 = 17	10 +10 = 20
18 +2 = 20	9 +9 = 18	16 +1 = 17	9 +7 = 16	12 +5 = 17	17 +2 = 19	Number Correct /20

Addition Test 4—Sums to 16, 17, 18, 19, and 20

15 +1 = 16	9 +7 = 16	5 +12 = 17	17 +2 = 19	8 +9 = 17	17 +1 = 18	8 +8 = 16
16 +3 = 19	18 +2 = 20	10 +7 = 17	15 +2 = 17	17 +3 = 20	9 +9 = 18	14 +2 = 16
19 +1 = 20	8 +10 = 18	13 +3 = 16	20 +0 = 20	7 +10 = 17	18 +1 = 19	Number Correct /20

135

Addition Test 5—Sums to 16, 17, 18, 19, and 20

17 +3 = 20	12 +5 = 17	9 +10 = 19	7 +10 = 17	10 +7 = 17	8 +8 = 16	12 +4 = 16
10 +10 = 20	8 +9 = 17	16 +2 = 18	17 +0 = 17	1 +16 = 17	10 +8 = 18	13 +7 = 20
7 +9 = 16	4 +12 = 16	15 +3 = 18	8 +10 = 18	10 +9 = 19	9 +9 = 18	Number Correct /20

Addition Test 6—Sums to 16, 17, 18, 19, and 20

9 +8 = 17	14 +6 = 20	5 +11 = 16	7 +12 = 19	15 +4 = 19	16 +1 = 17	3 +17 = 20
19 +1 = 20	10 +8 = 18	16 +3 = 19	13 +4 = 17	8 +8 = 16	10 +7 = 17	8 +11 = 19
9 +9 = 18	11 +6 = 17	14 +5 = 19	2 +15 = 17	7 +13 = 20	15 +2 = 17	Number Correct /20

136

Addition Test 7—Sums to 16, 17, 18, 19, and 20

13 +4 = 17	10 +7 = 17	12 +5 = 17	16 +2 = 18	2 +14 = 16	9 +10 = 19	12 +4 = 16
9 +11 = 20	8 +9 = 17	13 +7 = 20	17 +2 = 19	10 +10 = 20	9 +8 = 17	11 +7 = 18
16 +2 = 18	11 +8 = 19	15 +3 = 18	8 +8 = 16	5 +12 = 17	9 +9 = 18	Number Correct /20

Addition Test 8—Sums to 16, 17, 18, 19, and 20

13 +3 = 16	18 +2 = 20	16 +1 = 17	10 +10 = 20	14 +4 = 18	10 +9 = 19	9 +9 = 18
17 +1 = 18	10 +8 = 18	14 +3 = 17	8 +8 = 16	19 +0 = 19	7 +9 = 16	10 +7 = 17
19 +1 = 20	17 +0 = 17	6 +10 = 16	9 +8 = 17	17 +2 = 19	16 +2 = 18	Number Correct /20

137

Addition Test 9—Sums to 16, 17, 18, 19, and 20

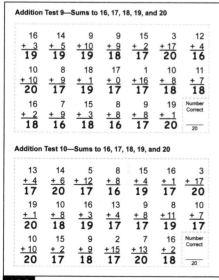

16 +3 = 19	14 +5 = 19	9 +10 = 19	9 +9 = 18	15 +2 = 17	3 +17 = 20	12 +4 = 16
10 +10 = 20	8 +9 = 17	18 +1 = 19	17 +0 = 17	1 +16 = 17	10 +8 = 18	11 +7 = 18
16 +2 = 18	7 +9 = 16	15 +3 = 18	8 +8 = 16	9 +8 = 17	19 +1 = 20	Number Correct /20

Addition Test 10—Sums to 16, 17, 18, 19, and 20

13 +4 = 17	14 +6 = 20	5 +12 = 17	8 +8 = 16	15 +4 = 19	16 +1 = 17	3 +17 = 20
19 +1 = 20	10 +8 = 18	16 +3 = 19	13 +4 = 17	9 +8 = 17	8 +11 = 19	10 +7 = 17
10 +10 = 20	15 +2 = 17	9 +9 = 18	2 +15 = 17	7 +13 = 20	16 +2 = 18	Number Correct /20

138

How Am I Doing?

Addition Tests—Sums to 1, 2, 3, 4, and 5

Number correct	Test 1	Test 2	Test 3	Test 4	Test 5	Test 6	Test 7	Test 8	Test 9	Test 10
20										
19										
18										
17										
16										
15										
14										
13										
12										
11										
10										
9										
8										
7										
6										
5										
4										
3										
2										
1										

Addition Tests—Sums to 6, 7, 8, 9, and 10

Number correct	Test 1	Test 2	Test 3	Test 4	Test 5	Test 6	Test 7	Test 8	Test 9	Test 10
20										
19										
18										
17										
16										
15										
14										
13										
12										
11										
10										
9										
8										
7										
6										
5										
4										
3										
2										
1										

139

How Am I Doing?

Addition Tests—Sums to 11, 12, 13, 14, and 15

Number correct	Test 1	Test 2	Test 3	Test 4	Test 5	Test 6	Test 7	Test 8	Test 9	Test 10
20										
19										
18										
17										
16										
15										
14										
13										
12										
11										
10										
9										
8										
7										
6										
5										
4										
3										
2										
1										

Addition Tests—Sums to 16, 17, 18, 19, and 20

Number correct	Test 1	Test 2	Test 3	Test 4	Test 5	Test 6	Test 7	Test 8	Test 9	Test 10
20										
19										
18										
17										
16										
15										
14										
13										
12										
11										
10										
9										
8										
7										
6										
5										
4										
3										
2										
1										

140

141

How to Use the Subtraction Table

The numbers in the dark border down the side show the rows. The numbers in the dark border at the top show the columns. You can use this table to subtract to find the difference of two numbers. For example, find the difference of 9 – 5.

Go down to the 9 row. Put your finger on the 9. Then slide your finger along the 9 row to the 5 column. The number in the square is your answer! So, 9 – 5 = 4.

If you find a blank space, that means you cannot subtract those two numbers.

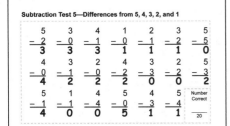

−	0	1	2	3	4	5	6	7	8	9	10
0	0										
1	1	0									
2	2	1	0								
3	3	2	1	0							
4	4	3	2	1	0						
5	5	4	3	2	1	0					
6	6	5	4	3	2	1	0				
7	7	6	5	4	3	2	1	0			
8	8	7	6	5	4	3	2	1	0		
9	9	8	7	6	5	4	3	2	1	0	
10	10	9	8	7	6	5	4	3	2	1	0

142

Subtraction Test 1—Differences from 5, 4, 3, 2, and 1

```
 5   4   2   5   4   3   1
-2  -3  -1  -4  -0  -3  -1
 3   1   1   1   4   0   0

 3   5   2   4   5   4   5
-0  -5  -2  -2  -1  -4  -3
 3   0   0   2   4   0   2

 4   2   3   1   3   5
-1  -0  -2  -0  -1
 3   2   1   1   2
```
Number Correct /20

Subtraction Test 2—Differences from 5, 4, 3, 2, and 1

```
 2   5   3   4   5   4   3
-1  -4  -2  -0  -3  -2  -0
 1   1   1   4   2   2   3

 5   4   5   1   3   2   4
-1  -1  -5  -1  -3  -0  -3
 4   3   0   0   0   2   1

 3   5   4   5   2   1
-1  -2  -4  -0  -2  -0
 2   3   0   5   0   1
```
Number Correct /20

143

Subtraction Test 3—Differences from 5, 4, 3, 2, and 1

```
 2   5   3   5   1   4   3
-2  -3  -1  -5  -0  -3  -2
 0   2   2   0   1   1   1

 5   1   4   2   3   2   5
-2  -1  -2  -1  -3  -0  -1
 3   0   2   1   0   2   4

 3   4   5   4   5   4
-0  -4  -0  -1  -4  -0
 3   0   5   3   1   4
```
Number Correct /20

Subtraction Test 4—Differences from 5, 4, 3, 2, and 1

```
 4   5   3   1   4   3   3
-4  -3  -2  -0  -3  -2  -1
 0   2   1   1   0   0   2

 5   2   5   1   3   1   2
-2  -1  -5  -1  -0  -1  -0
 3   1   0   3   3   0   2

 4   5   4   5   4   5
-3  -0  -0  -1  -2  -4
 1   5   4   4   2   1
```
Number Correct /20

144

Subtraction Test 5—Differences from 5, 4, 3, 2, and 1

```
 5   3   4   1   2   3   5
-2  -0  -1  -0  -1  -2  -5
 3   3   3   1   1   1   0

 4   3   2   4   3   2   5
-0  -1  -0  -2  -3  -2  -3
 4   2   2   2   0   0   2

 5   1   4   5   4   5
-1  -1  -4  -0  -3  -4
 4   0   0   5   1   1
```
Number Correct /20

Subtraction Test 6—Differences from 5, 4, 3, 2, and 1

```
 4   5   2   5   4   1   3
-0  -4  -2  -1  -1  -0  -1
 4   1   0   4   3   1   2

 2   3   5   3   1   4   3
-0  -2  -5  -0  -1  -2  -3
 2   1   0   3   0   2   0

 5   4   5   4   5   2
-3  -4  -2  -3  -0  -1
 2   0   3   1   5   1
```
Number Correct /20

145

Subtraction Test 7—Differences from 5, 4, 3, 2, and 1

```
 4   3   5   3   2   4   1
-1  -1  -4  -1  -0  -2  -0
 3   0   1   1   2   1   1

 5   2   1   5   5   4   3
-0  -2  -1  -3  -0  -0  -0
 5   0   0   2   0   0   3

 3   4   5   4   2   5
-1  -2  -2  -0  -1  -1
 2   2   3   4   1   4
```
Number Correct /20

Subtraction Test 8—Differences from 5, 4, 3, 2, and 1

```
 4   5   3   1   5   4   3
-4  -3  -2  -0  -4  -2  -1
 0   2   1   1   1   0   2

 5   2   5   1   3   5   4
-2  -1  -0  -1  -0  -5  -2
 3   1   5   3   3   0   2

 5   4   1   2   3   4
-1  -3  -0  -0  -3  -0
 4   1   0   2   0   4
```
Number Correct /20

146

Subtraction Test 9—Differences from 5, 4, 3, 2, and 1

```
 3   4   5   2   1   5   4
-3  -0  -5  -1  -0  -2  -1
 0   4   0   1   1   3   3

 4   3   2   5   3   1   3
-4  -1  -0  -3  -0  -1  -1
 0   2   2   2   3   0   2

 5   4   5   2   5   4
-1  -3  -0  -2  -4  -2
 4   1   5   0   1   2
```
Number Correct /20

Subtraction Test 10—Differences from 5, 4, 3, 2, and 1

```
 5   4   3   2   1   3   5
-4  -1  -3  -1  -0  -2  -3
 1   3   0   1   1   1   2

 2   3   5   4   2   4   5
-2  -0  -2  -0  -0  -2  -5
 0   3   3   4   2   2   0

 5   4   3   1   4   5
-0  -3  -1  -0  -1  -1
 5   1   2   0   0   4
```
Number Correct /20

147

Subtraction Test 1—Differences from 10, 9, 8, 7, and 6

```
10   8   6   7  10   9   6
-9  -6  -3  -4  -2  -6  -2
 1   2   3   3   8   3   4

 7  10   9   8   6   7  10
-7  -5  -8  -3  -5  -3  -1
 0   5   1   5   1   4   9

 8   6  10   9   7   8
-7  -0  -8  -5  -1  -2
 1   6   2   4   6   6
```
Number Correct /20

Subtraction Test 2—Differences from 10, 9, 8, 7, and 6

```
10   8   9   7  10   8   8
-6  -4  -2  -0  -3  -4  -1
 4   4   7   7   7   2   7

 6   7   8  10   7   9  10
-6  -2  -5  -4  -5  -1  -7
 0   5   3   6   2   8   3

 8   9   7   8   9  10
-8  -3  -6  -0  -7 -10
 0   6   1   8   2   0
```
Number Correct /20

148

Subtraction Test 3—Differences from 10, 9, 8, 7, and 6

```
 9  10   8   9   6   9   7
-4  -0  -3  -0  -4  -9  -7
 5  10   5   9   2   0   0

 8  10   7   6   9   8  10
-6  -8  -2  -3  -7  -2  -1
 2   2   5   3   2   6   9

10   6  10   9   8   7
-7  -1 -10  -6  -1  -5
 3   5   0   3   7   2
```
Number Correct /20

Subtraction Test 4—Differences from 10, 9, 8, 7, and 6

```
10   6   7  10   8   9   7
-4  -0  -3  -9  -4  -2  -4
 6   6   4   1   4   7   3

 6   8  10   9   7   9  10
-2  -5  -3  -5  -6  -1  -0
 4   3   7   4   1   8   7

 9  10   7   6   8   6
-3  -2  -1  -5  -7  -6
 6   8   6   1   1   0
```
Number Correct /20

149

Subtraction Test 5—Differences from 10, 9, 8, 7, and 6

```
10   8   9  10   8   9  10
-5  -8  -0  -6  -0  -4  -0
 5   0   9   4   8   5  10

 9   7   9   6  10   7   8
-8  -3  -9  -0  -3  -5  -1
 1   4   0   6   7   2   7

 7   9   6  10   8   7
-6  -7  -2  -8  -3  -2
 1   2   4   2   5   5
```
Number Correct /20

Subtraction Test 6—Differences from 10, 9, 8, 7, and 6

```
 9  10   8   6   7  10   9
-1  -4  -5  -6  -0  -7  -5
 8   6   3   0   7   3   4

 8   6  10   7   9   8   7
-2  -3  -1  -4  -6  -4  -0
 6   3   9   3   3   4   7

 6   9   6   8  10   9
-4  -8  -1  -7  -5  -0
 2   1   5   1   5   9
```
Number Correct /20

Subtraction Test 7—Differences from 10, 9, 8, 7, and 6
```
 8   10    8    9   10    9    7
-0   -9   -6   -2   -6   -4   -1
 8    1    2    7    4    5    6

 6    9    8    6    9   10    8
-5   -3   -8   -2   -9   -2   -1
 1    6    0    4    0    8    7

 7    9    6   10    8    7
-7   -0   -6  -10   -3   -4
 0    9    0    0    5    3
```
Number Correct ___ /20

Subtraction Test 8—Differences from 10, 9, 8, 7, and 6
```
 6    8    7   10    7    9    6
-3   -4   -5   -6   -0   -2   -1
 3    4    2    4    7    7    5

 7    6   10    8    9    6    7
-2   -5   -1   -5   -4   -0   -6
 5    1    9    3    5    6    1

 8    9    7    9   10    9
-7   -5   -3   -6   -8   -1
 1    4    4    3    2    8
```
Number Correct ___ /20

150

Subtraction Test 9—Differences from 10, 9, 8, 7, and 6
```
10    7    9    8    6   10    8
-7   -1   -3   -2   -4   -5   -8
 3    6    6    6    2    5    0

 9    8    6    7   10    9    8
-7   -0   -2   -7   -4   -8   -1
 2    8    4    0    6    1    7

10    9    7   10    8   10
-3   -9   -3   -2   -3   -0
 7    0    4    8    5   10
```
Number Correct ___ /20

Subtraction Test 10—Differences from 10, 9, 8, 7, and 6
```
10    8    9    8    6   10    8
-10  -2   -6   -7   -4   -1   -1
 0    6    3    1    2    9    7

 6    9   10    7    8    9   10
-0   -1   -8   -2   -5   -0   -4
 6    8    2    5    3    9    6

10    8    9    6   10    6
-5   -6   -1   -5   -7   -5
 5    2    5    1    3    1
```
Number Correct ___ /20

151

Subtraction Test 1—Differences from 15, 14, 13, 12, and 11
```
11   14   12   15   12   13   15
-0   -6   -8   -7   -5   -2   -9
11    8    4    8    7   11    6

13   11   15   13   14   15   11
-8  -10   -6   -9   -1   -5   -2
 5    1    9    4   13   10    9

15   12   14   11   13   11
-2   -0   -7   -3   -7   -8
13   12    7    8    6    3
```
Number Correct ___ /20

Subtraction Test 2—Differences from 15, 14, 13, 12, and 11
```
15   14   13   12   11   15   13
-1   -4   -2   -6   -5   -2   -1
14   10   11    6    6   13   12

14   11   12   13   15   11   12
-2   -3   -1   -5   -9   -1   -4
12    8   11    8    6   10    8

13   12   11   15   14   13
-10  -8   -4   -6   -5   -7
 3    4    7    9    9    6
```
Number Correct ___ /20

152

Subtraction Test 3—Differences from 15, 14, 13, 12, and 11
```
13   15   12   14   11   14   15
-0   -7   -6   -4   -9   -7   -5
13    8    6   10    2    7   10

14   11   15   13   14   15   11
-6   -3   -2   -3   -2   -1   -2
 8    8   13   10   12   14    9

15   12   14   11   13   11
-8   -8   -9   -7   -2   -4
 7    4    5    4   11    7
```
Number Correct ___ /20

Subtraction Test 4—Differences from 15, 14, 13, 12, and 11
```
11   12   13   14   15   11   13
-9   -4   -2   -6   -5   -2   -1
 2    8   11    8   10    9   12

12   11   12   13   15   11   12
-10  -3   -1   -6   -8   -5   -7
 2    8   11    7    7    6    5

13   12   11   15   14   13
-7   -8  -10   -6   -5   -4
 6    4    1    9    9    9
```
Number Correct ___ /20

153

Subtraction Test 5—Differences from 15, 14, 13, 12, and 11
```
15   13   11   12   14   12   14
-7   -5   -5   -1   -5   -6   -6
 8    8    6   11    9    6    8

11   13   14   15   13   14   11
-9  -10   -7   -1   -2   -3   -3
 2    3    7   14   11   11    8

12   15   14   11   13   11
-3  -10   -4   -7   -6   -1
 9    5   10    4    7   10
```
Number Correct ___ /20

Subtraction Test 6—Differences from 15, 14, 13, 12, and 11
```
14   12   11   13   15   12   13
-1   -4   -6   -7   -6   -2   -9
13    8    5    6    9   10    4

15   13   14   12   13   11   15
-2   -3   -8   -9   -2   -4   -7
13   10    6    3   11    7    8

13   11   12   15   14   13
-1   -2   -3   -5   -4  -10
12    9    9   10   10    3
```
Number Correct ___ /20

154

Subtraction Test 7—Differences from 15, 14, 13, 12, and 11
```
12   14   12   15   12   13   15
-4  -10  -12   -9   -5   -3   -7
 8    4    0    6    7   10    8

15   12   15   13   14   11   12
-2  -10   -8   -2   -6   -4   -1
13    2    7   11    8    7   11

14   15   13   11   13   15
-5  -10   -6   -7   -5   -5
 9    5    7    4    8   10
```
Number Correct ___ /20

Subtraction Test 8—Differences from 15, 14, 13, 12, and 11
```
13   14   15   12   11   15   13
-1   -4   -2   -6   -7  -12   -7
12   10   13    6    4    3    6

14   11   12   13   15   11   12
-2   -3   -1   -9   -9   -1   -4
12    8   11    4    6   10    8

12   15   13   15   14   13
-9   -8   -4   -6   -5   -0
 3    7    9    9    9   13
```
Number Correct ___ /20

155

Subtraction Test 9—Differences from 15, 14, 13, 12, and 11
```
15   13   12   15   14   11   15
-6   -5   -8   -1   -7  -10   -9
 9    8    4   14    7    1    6

12   11   15   14   13   15   14
-9   -7   -2   -9   -7   -5   -1
 3    4   13    5    6   10   13

11   13   14   15   13   12
-3   -9   -2   -7   -1   -2
 8    4   12    8   12   10
```
Number Correct ___ /20

Subtraction Test 10—Differences from 15, 14, 13, 12, and 11
```
15   14   13   12   11   13   15
-6   -4   -2   -6   -2  -10   -1
 9   10   11    6    9    3   14

14   13   12   11   15   11   12
-2   -3   -1  -10   -7   -1   -4
12   10   11    1    8   10    8

13   12   11   15   14   13
-6   -8   -4   -2   -5   -7
 7    4    7   13    9    6
```
Number Correct ___ /20

156

Subtraction Test 1—Differences from 20, 19, 18, 17, and 16
```
19   18   20   17   16   18   17
-9   -2   -1   -1   -7   -5   -7
10   16   19   16    9   13   10

17   18   17   20   16   18   19
-1   -8   -9   -2   -9  -10   -1
16   10    8   18    7    8   18

17   20   18   16   18   19
-2  -10   -9   -8   -1   -2
15   10    9    8   17   17
```
Number Correct ___ /20

Subtraction Test 2—Differences from 20, 19, 18, 17, and 16
```
20   16   19   17   18   16   17
-1  -10   -2   -1   -1   -2   -9
19    6   17   16   17   14    8

18   19   16   18   19   20   17
-2   -1   -8  -10   -9  -10   -7
16   18    8    8   10   10   10

16   17   20   16   17   18
-1   -2   -2   -6   -5   -9
15   15   18   10   12    9
```
Number Correct ___ /20

157

Subtraction Test 3—Differences from 20, 19, 18, 17, and 16
```
16   20   19   17   18   16   17
-6   -1   -9   -1   -9   -2   -7
10   19   10   16    9   14   10

18   19   17   20   16   18   17
-10 -10  -10   -2   -8   -2   -9
 8    9    7   18    8   16    8

19   16   20   18   19   17
-2   -7  -10   -8  -11   -2
17    9   10   10    8   15
```
Number Correct ___ /20

Subtraction Test 4—Differences from 20, 19, 18, 17, and 16
```
16   18   19   20   16   18   17
-1   -9   -2   -2   -6   -2   -9
15    9   17   18   10   16    8

17   16   19   18   19   17   20
-2  -10   -1   -8   -9   -1   -1
15    6   18   10   10   16   19

18   20   16   19   17   16
-1  -10   -8  -10   -7   -0
17   10    8    9   10   16
```
Number Correct ___ /20

158

Subtraction Test 5—Differences from 20, 19, 18, 17, and 16

```
 19   17   18   16   20   19   16
 -9   -2   -8   -9  -10   -2   -8
 10   15   10    7   10   17    8

 20   18   16   19   17   16   18
 -1   -1   -7  -10   -8  -12  -10
 19   17    9    9    9    4    8

 19   16   17   18   16   17
 -1   -6   -7   -9   -1  -11          Number Correct
 18   10   10    9   15    6              /20
```

Subtraction Test 6—Differences from 20, 19, 18, 17, and 16

```
 19   16   18   17   18   20   16
 -1   -8   -2   -9  -10   -2   -1
 18    8   16    8    8   18   15

 16   17   20   18   19   16   17
 -2  -12  -17   -9   -9   -9   -2
 14    5    3    9   10    7   15

 16   18   17   17   20   17
-10   -8   -7   -7  -10   -1          Number Correct
  6   10   10    9   10   16              /20
```

Subtraction Test 7—Differences from 20, 19, 18, 17, and 16

```
 20   19   17   16   18   19   17
-10   -2   -8   -9   -1  -10   -9
 10   17    9    7   17    9    8

 18   16   19   17   20   18   16
 -8  -10   -9   -2  -14  -10   -1
 10    6   10   15    6    8   15

 19   18   17   18   16   20
-12  -15   -7   -9  -14  -15          Number Correct
  7    3   10    9    2    5              /20
```

Subtraction Test 8—Differences from 20, 19, 18, 17, and 16

```
 16   17   18   20   18   17   16
 -1   -9   -2  -13   -9   -2   -8
 15    8   16    7    9   15    8

 17   16   19   16   19   20   18
-12  -10   -9   -7   -2  -19  -10
  5    6   10    9   17    1    8

 18   20   16   18   17   16
 -1  -10   -9   -8   -7  -16          Number Correct
 17   10    7   10   10    0              /20
```

Subtraction Test 9—Differences from 20, 19, 18, 17, and 16

```
 18   19   16   17   16   19   16
 -9   -2   -8   -7  -10   -9   -6
  9   17    8   10    9    9   10

 20   16   19   18   17   20   18
-10  -10   -9   -8   -9   -2   -1
 10    6   10   10    8   18   17

 17   20   18   16   19   18
 -8   -1  -10  -12   -1   -7          Number Correct
  9   19    8    4   18   11              /20
```

Subtraction Test 10—Differences from 20, 19, 18, 17, and 16

```
 18   17   19   20   19   16   17
 -1   -8   -2   -8   -9   -7   -1
 17    9   17   12   10    9   16

 19   16   17   18   16   20   18
-10   -9  -10   -8   -6  -15  -10
  9    7    7   10   10    5    8

 17   16   18   19   20   17
 -7   -8   -9   -5  -13   -9          Number Correct
 10    8    9   14    7    8              /20
```

159   160   161

354

Grammar and Reading

What Is a Sentence? p. 190
1. Students should use a checkmark for a), d), and f). Students should use Xs to mark b), c), and e).
2. Check that students have written complete sentences.

Exploring Kinds of Sentences, p. 191
1. a) question mark, b) period, c) exclamation mark, d) question mark, e) period, f) exclamation mark, g) question mark
2. Sample answers:
   a) John is walking his dog.   Amy is reading a book.
   b) Are you ready to go?   Do you like apples?
   c) I like to go bike riding!   I love my teddy bear!
   d) Finish your homework.   Look at that rainbow!

Making a Noun Collage, p. 193
Ensure that students have chosen noun pictures. You might want to create a display of students' collages.

Nouns: Am I a Person, Place, or Thing? p. 194
1. People nouns in red: girl, teacher, student, grandma
   Place nouns in blue: home, beach, backyard, farm, park
   Thing nouns in green: yo-yo, fork, pencil, dog, toy, blanket, cheese

Proper Nouns Need a Capital Letter, p. 195
1. Sample answers: a) Max, b) Monday
2. Sample answers: Jenny, Ontario, Friday

Plural Nouns, p. 196
1. a) cats, b) birds, c) pigs, d) eggs, e) kids, f) bells, g) nests, h) jobs
2. a) people, b) men, c) teeth
3. a) witches, b) wishes, c) glasses, d) rashes, e) buses, f) lunches, g) boxes, h) dishes

Making a Verb Collage, p. 198
Ensure that students have chosen pictures that represent verbs. You might want to create a display of students' collages.

Compound Words, p. 199
1. a) butterfly, b) cupcake, c) backpack, d) football, e) sunshine, f) snowball, g) bullfrog
2. Answers will vary. You might wish to have students share their words with the class.

Using Text Features—Table of Contents, p. 203
1. The title of the book is Farm Animals.
2. Farmer Brown is the author.
3. There are 6 chapters in the book.
4. Chapter 5's title is Horses.
5. Chapter 2's title is Chickens.
6. Chapter 6 tells about the barn.
7. Chapter 4 tells about cows.
8. Chapter 3 is about pigs.

Can We Get a Dog? p. 205
1. Andrew is trying to get his parents to get a dog.
2. B. a letter
3. Andrew's family can get a dog at the shelter.
4. Students should choose any three of the following arguments Andrew uses: Every dog needs a good home. We can get one at the shelter. I promise to take care of it. A dog is a good pet for us to love.
5. Yes, I think he did. He gives good reasons why the family would love a dog and he says he will take care of it.

Write a Letter, p. 207
You might wish to have students share their letters with the class.

My New Boots, p. 208
1. Kim has new boots.
2. The rain boots are as red as a fire truck and as shiny as a dime.
3. Kim likes to wear her boots when she splashes in puddles.
4. Kim's boots get wet but she stays dry.
5. Sample answers: cherries, tomatoes, flowers
6. Sample answer: winter boots

My Trip to a Farm, p. 210
1. Kyle wrote the email.
2. Kyle's grandma will get the email.
3. Kyle is telling the story. Kyle tells what he did at the farm.
4. Kyle went to a farm.
5. Students should draw a pie.

Little Brother, Big Brother, p. 212
1. Rob is 5 years older than Tim.
2. Dan is twelve.
3. Sample answer: Rob probably makes silly sounds and silly faces to make Tim smile.
4. Sample answer: Dan might take Andy's toys away or tease him.
5. Answers will vary. You might with to ask students to share with the class.

A Hole in My Sock, p. 214
1. The L stands for Lucy.
2. The hole got big.
3. Lucy tried to fix the hole with tape.
4. Lucy could have had her mother mend her sock when she got home.
5. Answers will vary. Sample answers: Lynn, Lynda, Lee, Lisa, Lori, Lexi
6. Answers will vary. You might wish to have students share their sock stories with the class.

Cookie Day, p. 216
1. Sara likes jam cookies, nut cookies, and sugar cookies.
2. Sara's dad says jam is too sweet.
3. Nuts make Sara's mom sick.
4. B. sugar
5. Everyone in my family can eat sugar cookies!

The Day My Cat Spoke, p. 218

1. The boy's name is Ben.
2. His cat's name is Abby.
3. A. surprised
4. The cat told the boy to get up.
5. Sample answers: amazing, great, terrific, super
6. Sample answer: I would be shocked and happy, and maybe a little scared.

Ice Cream Fun, p. 220

1. Answers will vary. You might wish to ask a few students to share their answers with the class.
2. Answers might vary. Students should include any three of the following: ice cream, a bowl, syrup, toppings, a spoon to eat with
3. First, put some ice cream into a bowl.
   Then, pour some syrup on it.
   Next, add some toppings.
   Finally, eat the ice cream!

Social Studies

What Is a Community? p. 239

1. city
2. street
3. school
4. everyone
5. community

Thinking About My Community, p. 240

1. Answers will vary.
2. Answers will vary.
3. You might wish to create a bulletin board display of students' drawings.
4. Answers might vary. Students will probably circle the van, bicycle, subway, foot, truck, car, bus, and airplane.
5. Answers will vary.
6. You might wish to create a bulletin board display of students' drawings.
7. Students will probably say they see stop signs, street name signs, and perhaps advertising signs.
8. Answers will vary. Students will probably say there are grocery stores, a pharmacy, pizza shops, and burger places in their community.
9. Answers will vary.
10. Answers might vary.
11. You might wish to create a bulletin board display of students' drawings.
12. Answers will vary. You might wish to have students share with the class.

Word Search—Places Found in Some Communities, p. 245

P	O	L	I	C	E	S	T	A	T	I	O	N	P	I
C	Q	H	O	M	E	S	T	I	W	P	C	P	H	W
I	Z	J	Z	L	E	J	U	Y	A	A	Y	L	O	Q
T	L	S	C	H	O	O	L	N	R	S	A	S	B
Y	M	Y	A	U	D	Z	R	J	L	K	B	Y	P	M
H	A	U	B	U	S	S	T	O	P	Y	U	G	I	U
A	L	R	A	I	R	P	O	R	T	B	Y	R	T	S
L	L	P	O	S	T	O	F	F	I	C	E	O	A	E
L	F	I	R	E	S	T	A	T	I	O	N	U	L	U
S	T	O	R	E	D	U	S	P	O	O	L	N	M	M
B	B	L	I	B	R	A	R	Y	W	K	K	D	X	Z

1. Answers will vary. You might wish to have students share with the class.

Needs and Wants, p. 246

1. Answers will vary. You might wish to have students share with the class.
2. Answers will vary. You might wish to have students share with the class.

Our Community Collage, p. 247

You might wish to create a bulletin board display of students' collages.

Keep Our Community Clean Poster, p. 248

You might wish to create a bulletin board display of students' posters.

Where Does the Trash Go? p. 249

1. Answers might vary. Sample answer: A landfill is a big place with a lot of dirt where they bury trash. I know because the text tells me and bottom picture shows me.
2. Answers might vary, but students should choose on of the following facts: Most trash goes to a landfill. Machines dig dirt to cover the trash. Landfills can get full.
3. The top picture shows a man picking up trash and dumping it into a garbage truck. The bottom picture shows a bulldozer moving the trash around in a landfill.
4. Teacher: My job is to teach children.
   Construction Worker: My job is to build buildings.

People in Our Community, p. 251

Postal Worker: My job is to deliver mail.
Police Officer: My job is to protect people.
Firefighter: My job is to put out fires.
Doctor: My job is to keep people healthy and to help sick people get better
Utility Worker: My job is to make sure people have electricity.
Sanitation Worker: My job is to keep the community clean.
Dentist: My job is to keep people's teeth healthy.

A Community Worker, p. 252
Answers will vary. You might wish to have students share with the class.

When I Grow Up..., p. 253
Answers will vary. You might wish to have students share with the class.

Staying Safe Poster, p. 254
1. To help children learn ways to stay safe.
2. You should wear a helmet when you ride a bike.
3. You should look both ways when you cross the street because cars come from both directions.
4. Answers might vary. Sample answers: You can use a crosswalk and point when you cross. You can cross where there is a crossing guard. You can cross with an adult or older child.
5. No.
6. No.

Help! p. 256
You might wish to have students share their drawings with the class.
1. Answers might vary. Students would probably say that someone needs help.
2. Water and a fire hose are used to put out fires. Some students might mention fire extinguishers.
3. A fire engine
4. In most areas, students should know to call 911.
5. Students should choose three of the following, or give their own ideas: if there is a fire, if someone is very sick or hurt, if someone is robbed, if someone needs help in a boat or on a mountain.

What Is a Smoke Detector? p. 258
1. A smoke detector tells you when there is smoke from something burning.
2. A smoke detector beeps very loudly.
3. The checklist helps me know exactly what to do if there is a fire and in what order I should do it.
4. First, go outside.
   Next, find an adult.
   Finally, ask for help.
5. False
6. True

Families Can Be Different, p. 260
Answers will vary. Talking about families can be sensitive for some students. You might wish to ask volunteers to share with the class.

Families Work Together, p. 262
Answers will vary. You might wish to ask students to share ideas with the class.

Growing Up, p. 263
1. Answers will vary.
2. Answers will vary.
3. Answers will vary. You might wish to have students share with the class.

4. The text says that next year I will be even bigger. I will also be taller next year. I will also know how to do more things.
5. Answers will vary.

How Have You Grown and Changed? p. 265
Sample answers:
My size: When I was little – I was smaller and shorter. Now – I am taller and bigger.
The food I eat: When I was little – I ate soft baby food and mashed foods. Now – I eat all kinds of foods that are not soft.
The toys I like: When I was little – I liked rattles and soft toys. Now – I like hard toys but I also like some soft ones. I like games and puzzles, too.
Where I sleep: When I was little – I slept in a crib. Now – I sleep in a bed.

Helping at Home, p. 266
1. Answers will vary. Students should choose any three of the following ways to help at home: make your bed, put your clothes away, keep you room neat, help your family carry bags, help set and clear the table.
2. Answers might vary. Students might say they can pick up their toys and put them away, clean up their clothes and put dirty clothes in the hamper, and that they can make their bed.
3. Answers will vary.
4. Answers will vary. Sample answer: I can help take dishes out of the dishwasher or put clean dishes and utensils away.
5. Answers might vary. Sample answer: I can help feed a pet or give it water. I can help brush the pet. I can help take the pet for a walk or play with it.

Cleaning Your Room, p. 268
1. Answers will vary.
2. Answers will vary. Sample answers: I keep my clothes in my dresser. I keep some of my clothes in my closet.
3. Answers might vary. Sample answers: Make my bed. Pick everything up off the floor. Throw out things that I do not need. Fold my clothes and put them away.
4. Answers will vary. Students might say they can give things they do not need to a little brother or sister or a friend, or donate them to a charity for other children to enjoy.
5. You might wish to have students share their drawings with the class.

You Can Help with a Baby, p. 270
1. Sample answers: A baby might cry if it gets scared or lonely, or if it is tired, hungry, bored, or it needs to be changed.
2. Answers will vary. You might wish to ask students to share with the class.
3. Answers will vary. Sample answers: rattles, squeaky toys, soft toys, toys that light up or make noise, toys they can safely put in their mouth.
4. Answers might vary. Sample answer: peek-a-boo or patty cake

Are You Ready? p. 272

1. Students should choose any two of the following: brush your teeth, get dressed, make your bed, comb your hair, eat breakfast.
2. Answers will vary. You might wish to have students share with the class.
3. Answers will vary.
4. Answers will vary. Students should say at least twice a day.
5. Answers will vary. You might wish to have students share with the class. Sample answers: pack my lunch, brush my hair, let my dog out, feed my fish, watch cartoons, play with my baby brother

What I Am Learning at School, p. 274

1. Answers will vary.
2. Answers will vary. Sample answer: It is important to be nice to others because I want to make friends and I want people to be nice to me.
3. Answers will vary. Sample answers: It is important to listen to other people because we can learn things from others. It is important to listen because if we do not, the person speaking cannot be heard.
4. Answers will vary.
5. Answers will vary. Sample answers: walk slowly so you do not slip or fall and hurt yourself, be careful when you are playing so you do not get hurt or hurt someone else, pay attention to the teacher so you will learn and know what to do.

Thinking About Rules, p. 276

Answers will vary. You might wish to have students suggest rules and you can list them on the board.

Science

Living Things, p. 277

1. All living things need food, water, and air.
2. Yes, because the squirrel grows, moves, and needs food, water, and air to live.
3. Students should circle the man, dog, cow, and flower.

Living Things Collage, p. 279

Sentences will vary, but should show an understanding that all living things grow, move, and need food, water, and air.

Non-living Things Collage, p. 280

Sentences will vary, but should show an understanding that all non-living things do not grow, move, or need food, water, or air.

My Body, p. 281

1.

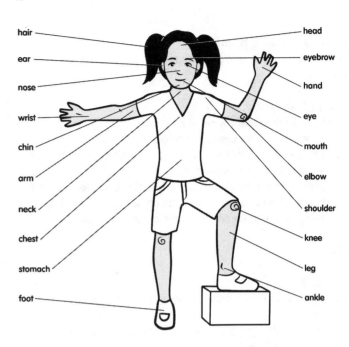

I Can Move My Body, p. 282

1. Sample answer: I think the boy in the picture is telling the story because he says "I can bend." so he is talking about himself.
2. The words *bend, turn,* and *stretch* describe ways the body can move.
3. The boy is bending his body over to the left side. He is stretching his right arm up high. He is stretching his right side over to the left.
4. Students should circle: A. TRUE. The text tells us the boy likes to move.

Baby Teeth, p. 284

1. Answers will vary.
2. Answers will vary.
3. Most children have 20 baby teeth at age three.
4. An adult tooth grows in after a baby tooth falls out.
5. When a tooth is ready to fall out, it moves.

Brush Your Teeth, p. 285

1. Brushing helps you stay well.
2. You should brush your teeth at least two times a day.
3. Answers will vary.
4. Students should number the steps in this order:
   - __3__ Make sure to brush all of your teeth.
   - __4__ Rinse your mouth with water.
   - __2__ Pour a little water on your toothbrush.
   - __1__ Put toothpaste on your toothbrush.

Clean Hands, p. 287

1. a) sick, b) soap, c) germs, d) eat, e) bathroom
2. Answers might vary. Students should mention that washing hands helps keep germs away, and that soap kills germs and helps keep you from getting sick.

Steps for Washing Hands, p. 288

1. First—Wet your hands under warm water.
2. Next—Cover your hands with soap.
3. Then—Scrub the soap all over your hands for 20 to 30 seconds.
4. After—Rinse the soap off under warm water.
5. Finally—Dry your hands.

Cover Sneezes and Coughs, p. 289

1. The title tells me I will be reading about covering sneezing and coughing.
2. When you sneeze or cough, you spread germs.
3. The pictures help me to know what happens when you sneeze. They show what happens when you do not use a tissue, and when you do use a tissue.
4. Students should list two of the following: You can use a tissue when you sneeze. You can cover your mouth when you cough. You can cough or sneeze into your sleeve if you do not have a tissue.
5. The author is trying to teach the reader how to not spread germs when they are sick.
6. Answers may vary. Sample answers: Some students might say "Bless you." Others might say "Gesundheit."

Growing Up, p. 291

1. Answers will vary. You might wish to create a bulletin board display of students' drawings.
2. Answers will vary.
3. Answers will vary, but students should indicate that they have grown taller and bigger, they eat different foods, they play with different toys, and they sleep in a bed instead of a crib.

Using Braille to Read Without Seeing, p. 293

Circulate around the room to see if students need help. Help students make the clay bumps, if necessary. After students make their names, you might wish to have them make a short message or a word or two in braille.

Animals On the Move, p. 294

1. a) rabbit, b) turtle, c) tiger, d) monkey

Comparing Living Things, p. 295

Answers will vary, depending on what two living things the student chooses to compare.

Brain Stretch, p. 296

Sample answer: A chipmunk gets air, food, water, and shelter from its environment.

About Seeds, p. 297

1. The text tells me a seed is a tiny plant waiting to grow.
2. Seeds need sun, water, and soil to grow.
3. The two special parts talked about in the text are fluff on dandelion seeds and wings on maple tree seeds.
4. Students should list two of the following types of seeds from the text: a peanut, a coconut, a dandelion seed with fluff on it, and a maple tree seed with wings on it.

5. The fact that we learned from the text is: A. Seeds need sun, water, and soil to grow.

Animals Live in Different Places, p. 299

1. a) moose—forest; b) duck—pond; c) whale—ocean; d) owl—tree; e) bee—hive

Goats and Sheep, p. 300

1. a) Yes, b) No, c) No
2. Goats like to reach up to eat leaves off trees.
3. Sheep eat grass and plants off the ground.

A Healthy Environment, p. 301

Ensure that students have labelled their drawings. You might wish to create a bulletin board display of drawings or have students share with the class.

People Affect Living Things, p. 302

1. Sample answer: Polluted water might make the fish sick or kill them.
2. Check that students' drawings show a way to help the environment.
3. Check that students' sentences tell something about their drawing.

Brain Stretch, p. 304

Students should say that food gives them the energy they need to grow.

What Is Energy? p. 306

1. jump
2. energy
3. create
4. Students should circle B, C, D, and F.

Where Energy Comes From, p. 306

1. Answers will vary.
2. You might wish to ask students to share their answers with the class.

We Get Energy From the Sun, p. 307

1. Drawings will vary, but should show what the Sun's light and heat do.

Experiment: How Does Sunlight Affect Plants? p. 308

1. Answers will vary, but students might say that the plant without sunlight will not grow.
2. Drawings should show that the plant in the sunlight is still healthy and green, whereas the plant in the dark is spindly, yellow, and almost dead.
3. Sample answer: The plant that did not get sunlight turned yellow, weak, and nearly died.
4. sunlight

We Get Energy From Food, p. 310

1. Labels, counterclockwise from the top: Sun, plants, animals, humans
2. a) Sun; b) energy; c) animals, plants

Healthy Foods Collage, p. 312

You might wish to create a bulletin board display of students' collages.

Farmers, p. 313

1. Farmers grow fruits and vegetables.
2. Meat comes from cows and chickens.
3. Truck drivers take the food to the stores.
4. Store clerks sell us the food.
5. Ensure that students' drawings show their family participating in cooking food together. Ensure that students write a sentence about their picture.

Brain Stretch, p. 315

Sample answers: toys, flashlight, radio, portable music player, cell phone, camera

Energy at Work, p. 315

1. a) battery; b) wind; c) gasoline; d) wood; e) electricity; f) Sun

Activity: Energy Matching Game, p. 317

1. a) wood—campfire, heat; b) electrical outlet—lamp, light; c) battery—radio, sound; d) wind—kite, movement

Saving Energy, p. 318

You might wish to create a bulletin board display of students' posters.

1. a) S, b) S, c) W, d) W, e) W
2. Answers will vary. You might wish to have students share their item and sentence with the class.

Objects Are Made From Materials, p. 320

1. Check that students have correctly identified the materials the objects are made from. You may wish to have students share their choices with the class.
2. Answers will vary.

Natural and Manufactured Materials, p. 322

1. Natural Materials: wool, tree sap, wood
   Materials Made by People: fabric, plastic, steel

Did You Know? p. 323

Sample answers: spoon, car, hammer, bicycle frame, legs on a desk, door handle

Where Do Materials Come From? p. 324

1. rubber—tree sap; fabric—cotton; steel—rock; paper—tree; wool—sheep

Light and Heat Affect What We Do, p. 325

You might wish to discuss this further with students and ask for ideas of what other activities light and heat would affect and in what ways. For example, what could they do on rainy days when there is no sunshine, or on snowy days when there is little heat?

Brain Stretch, p. 326

Students should circle the fan and draw a square around the thermostat.

What Is It Like Outside? p. 326

1. sunny—sunglasses; rainy—umbrella; snowy—mittens; windy—kite; cool—jacket
2. a) cold; b) hot; c) cool; d) cold; e) hot; f) warm; g) cold; h) cool; i) warm

The Seasons Affect What We Do, p. 328

1. a) winter, b) spring, c) fall, d) summer
2. Students should circle (a) building the snowman, which can only be done in winter.
3. Sample answer: Swimming can be done indoors in winter.

My Favourite Season, p. 330

Answers will vary. Ensure that students identify their favourite season and give three reasons why they like it best. You might wish to have students share with the class.